Polly Pinder's

PAPERCRAFTS

Creative projects using paper and card

For the staff and students of the Graphic Design Section,
Wakefield College.

Polly Pinder's
PAPERCRAFTS

Creative projects using paper and card

SEARCH PRESS

First published in Great Britain 1994

Search Press Limited
Wellwood, North Farm Road,
Tunbridge Wells, Kent TN2 3DR

ISBN 0 85532 661 1

Colour separated by P&W Graphics, Singapore
Printed in Spain by Salingraf SAL., Bilbao

Contents

Introduction

Paper must be one of the most versatile products ever invented by man. A brief look at its history tells us that the Egyptians developed a type of paper over 5,000 years ago. They used papyrus, a reed which still grows on the banks of the Nile. The reeds were split, woven into sheets, and dampened, then beaten flat and polished. Paper as we know it today, made from pulp, was produced in the second century BC by the Chinese. From there it spread via trading routes throughout the world and eventually, in the late fifteenth century, it came to England. All paper was handmade until 1798, when a machine for producing a continuous roll was invented by the French. The machine was brought to England in 1803.

Paper is a thin, flexible substance made from the pulped cellulose fibres of wood, grasses or rags. It can be produced in different weights: from wafer-thin sheets, as flimsy as finely woven silk, to several sheets bonded together to make a less flexible card. Today paper is one of the world's most widely used substances. Apart from books, magazines and newspapers that we read, paper is used to write on, to wrap things, to cover walls – the list is endless.

In this book I have attempted to introduce you to a wide range of papercrafts, from simple windmills to intricate paper lanterns. I like to recycle paper: wallpaper samples, photographs from magazines, old greetings cards, etc., when I can, but I also make use of a wide variety of new papers.

I like *everything* to be thoroughly explained. I admit to being easily confused, even by very basic directions, and I tend to assume that everyone is like me. I hope that the way the instructions are presented in this book will enable children, as well as adults, to achieve a successful result with many of the projects. Those readers who are adept in the craft skills area will, I trust, forgive the detailed or reiterated instructions.

Using the premise that if you are going to do something you may as well make a good job of it, only four things are needed to attain this end. The most important is the *desire* to produce something which is beautifully crafted (however simple) and which, if given as a gift, will be long treasured. You will also need *confidence*, which I hope that I am offering now, and which also comes with practice. The last two are *patience* and *care*. Good basic equipment could also be added to the list.

We are all capable of achieving much more than we imagine, so do not ever be limited by what you think you cannot do; believe that you can do it, and you will.

Paper is a wonderful material to work with. It comes in a multitude of colours, textures, weights and qualities.

Materials

Although most of the work in this book has been produced with 'second use' papers (wallpaper, wrapping paper, cartons, etc.), a few of the textured papers are not widely available to the public – they are generally supplied to printers and companies who require large quantities (and here I would like to thank paper merchants G.H. Smith, Brands and Wiggins Teape for their samples). However, there is certainly a much greater variety being sold in art and craft shops than was the case several years ago.

In order to accumulate a rich assortment of papers and card, I suggest that a spare drawer or cupboard (is there such a thing in any house?) or, failing that, a sturdy box, be used for the sole purpose of storing interesting bits and pieces which may come your way. Christmas and birthdays are a good time for adding to the box: it seems such a shame to discard the beautiful packaging and wrapping used to enclose our gifts.

Basic equipment

I have listed basic materials and equipment at the beginning of each chapter, then given a more specific list for each subject. What you will certainly need is something to cut with and cut on and a method of sticking.

Cutting tools

There are many craft knives on the market: some have clip-on blades held on metal or plastic handles; others have a length of blade hidden within the handle which is pushed out, then snapped off when a new one is required. I prefer the simple, slim, metal-handled type which has removable blades (careful handling is needed when replacing these). There is nothing more discouraging than trying to cut with a blunt or damaged blade so it is wise to keep a small stock in hand.

Scissors are essential and, as with all tools, quality pays; so buy the best you can afford – stainless-steel ones if possible. They should be small with pointed blades, have a smooth snipping motion and be comfortable on the fingers. Keep them just for your papercrafts.

Cutting mats are not cheap but with ordinary use (if you do not hack or chip at them) they will last almost indefinitely. I would suggest investing in a good size mat, say 300 x 450mm (12 x 18in), which will cost only a little more than a much smaller one. When cutting straight lines use a steel-edged perspex rule.

Glues and adhesives

Methods of sticking are a personal matter. Double-sided sticky tape (I refer to this as DSST throughout the book) is invaluable. Ordinary sticky tape and masking tape are also needed. Large areas can be stuck with a variety of glues: Cow Gum is a brand of colourless rubber solution which I like and use regularly despite the fact that it is highly flammable and somewhat fumy; solid, non-toxic glue sticks are quite adequate though they can cause thin paper to distort because of their water content; I never use spray adhesives (they are banned in many studios) because they are both messy and dangerous – the tiny particles of glue can be inhaled unless a protective mask is worn; dry adhesive, the latest

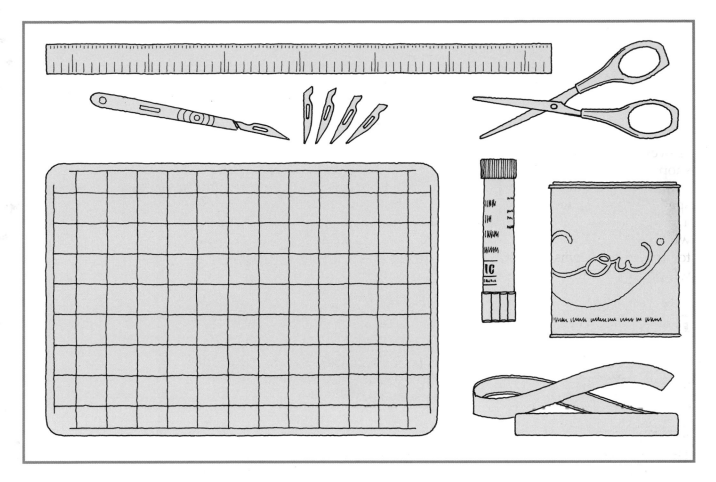

newcomer to the sticking scene, comes in sheets and is extremely economical, clean and easy to apply. I tend to use a combination of Cow Gum, glue stick and dry adhesive, whichever is most appropriate for the job. All of the above items can be bought at most art and craft shops, as can the other materials and equipment listed in the book.

Design sources

Being a devotee of the arts and crafts movement, I loudly proclaim the wisdom of encouraging and perpetuating hand skills and am inclined, in my exuberance, to dismiss all technology. This is a mistake, because as we know, it has its place. The use of the photocopier (a very useful tool for creating interesting images) is a case in point. One of my students recently photocopied the top half of his jeans for a graphic design project. Various effects can be achieved using combinations of your own drawings or sketches and photographs or pictures cut from magazines. If you have access to some form of technology, use it as a tool for your creativity.

windmills

Pinwheels

The pinwheels opposite are very simple to create and can be made from plain coloured paper, though double-sided paper gives a much jollier effect. Gift wrapping paper, coloured writing paper and coloured cartridge paper were used to construct the three basic shapes: a single pinwheel made from a square; a double pinwheel made from two triangles; and a double-flower pinwheel made from two circles.

It is not known whether pinwheels are a toy derivation of real windmills, but they probably originated in Japan. They are not, strictly speaking, origami, because glue is needed to hold the folded sections in place, but apart from this, they have all the simple qualities of the art of Japanese paper-folding.

Materials and equipment

Coloured papers; Cow Gum; a palette knife; double-sided sticky tape (DSST); scissors; a craft knife; a steel-edged rule; a pencil and eraser; 8mm ($^5/_{16}$in) dowel cut into 360mm (14in) lengths (for the handles); sturdy drawing pins; a small hammer; and a compass (to draw the circles for the flower pinwheel).

To make the double-sided papers, choose two contrasting (patterned and plain) or complementary colour schemes. You will need four papers for the double pinwheels. Cut the papers roughly to shape and coat the underside of each with a thin film of glue. Leave until almost dry, then stick firmly together. In all cases it will be prudent to make a trial wheel from cheap cartridge paper before embarking on one made with expensive wrapping paper (the foils, though very attractive, are usually more costly than the patterned papers).

Single pinwheel

1. Cut a 150mm (6in) square.
2. Lightly draw lines from two corners to the opposite corners.

3. Make a 75mm (3in) cut from each corner. Make a pencil mark at the centre point, then rub the lines out.

4. Cut and attach pieces of DSST to each alternate corner, then carefully bend the corner over and stick it against the centre point. Make a hole in the centre with the drawing pin.

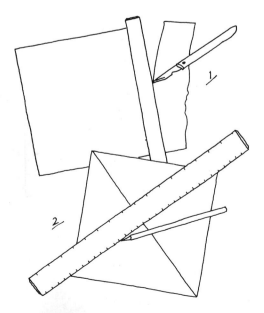

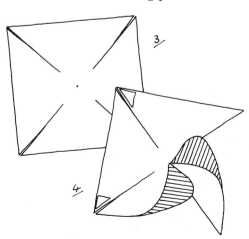

Gift wrap, writing and cartridge paper have been stuck together to make these jolly double-sided pinwheels.

13

5. Cut a strip of paper (using one of the papers from which the wheel is made) just a fraction longer than the dowel and 35mm (1³/₈in) wide. Stick DSST along both edges, then wrap firmly round the dowel.

6. Make a hole with a pin 10mm (³/₈in) from the top (the seam should be at the back). Attach the wheel firmly, using a hammer, but leave enough room for the wheel to spin freely. Cut a circle from one of the papers large enough to cover the drawing pin. Attach with DSST.

Double pinwheel

1. Cut two equal-sided triangles, one with 225mm (9in) sides and the other with 175mm (7in) sides.

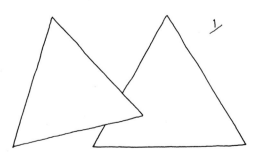

2. Measure and mark a point exactly halfway along each side, then draw a faint line from each point to the opposite corner.

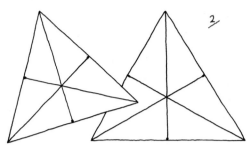

3. Make a 100mm (4in) cut from each corner of the large triangle and an 75mm (3in) cut from each corner of the smaller one. Make a pencil mark on the centre point of each triangle and rub out the lines. Make a hole through the pencil mark with the drawing pin.

4. Attach a piece of DSST to each alternate corner of each triangle.

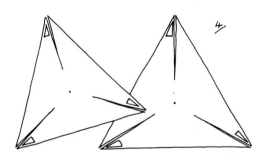

5. Stick pieces of DSST around the pin hole of the larger triangle. Push the drawing pin through the hole from the back. Lay the small triangle on top, as shown in the drawing. Remove the pin and press the two firmly together in the middle.

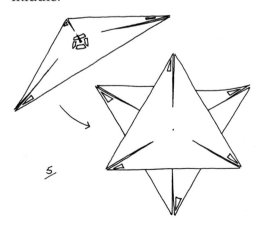

6. Carefully fold each alternate corner of the small triangle over and stick against the pin hole. Repeat with the large triangle.

7. Follow steps 5 and 6 of the single pinwheel instructions (see page 14) to cover and attach the handle.

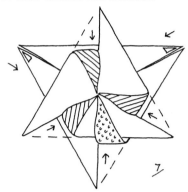

Double-flower pinwheel

This may sound complex but it is simple if you read through the instructions first, following the corresponding drawings at the same time.

1. Draw a circle with a radius (the distance from the centre point to the edge of the circle) of 100mm (4in).

2. Keeping the compass at the same measurement, divide the circle into six equal, curved sections – place the compass point anywhere on the drawn circle and swing the compass round, lightly drawing a curved line to the centre. Now put the compass point on the edge of the circle where the line has just been drawn and make another section. Repeat until the six sections have been made.

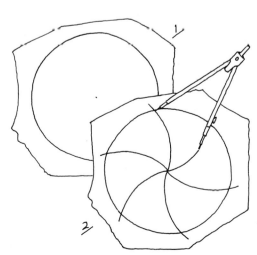

3. Lightly draw another circle from the centre with a radius of 25mm (1in).

4. Cut round the large circle, then cut curves in to the edge of the inner circle.

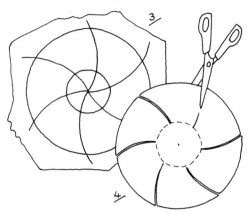

5. Attach pieces of DSST to the longest corners of each section then carefully fold them over and stick to the opposite corners.

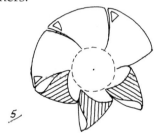

6. Repeat steps 1 to 4 for the small flower which will go in the centre – drawing the outer circle with a radius of 70mm (2³/₄ in) and the inner one with a radius of 15mm (⁵/₈ in).

7. Attach pieces of DSST to the longest corner of each section then carefully fold over and stick against the pin hole.

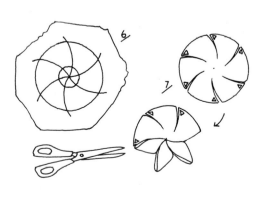

8. Attach pieces of DSST round the pin hole of the large flower. Stick the pin through the back of the flower then manoeuvre the small flower on to the pin so that the petals sit snugly between those of the large flower. Remove the pin and press the two firmly together in the centre.

9. Follow steps 5 and 6 of the single pinwheel instructions (see page 14) to cover and attach the handle.

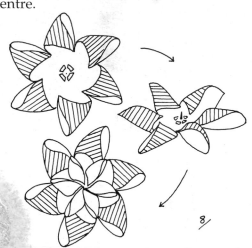

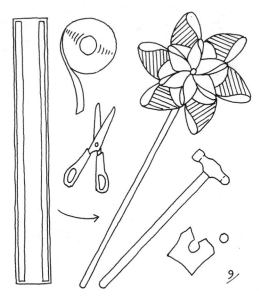

Windmills

The little wooden windmill (opposite left) is based on the design of early Dutch smock mills – so called because they appeared to resemble a miller wearing his traditional smock. The top section or 'cap' was turned into the wind (in order to achieve maximum power from the wind) by the miller pulling a chain which hung from the back of the cap. This turned a gearwheel running on a curved rack which was fixed to the top of the tower wall.

The brick windmill (opposite right) is based very loosely on one of several Norfolk mills still in use today. Purist model-makers may shudder at the term 'loosely'. Their perfect replications of historic buildings deserve the greatest praise and admiration, but simply looking at a building and taking manageable elements of the design for your model is just as acceptable and rewarding.

Modelling other buildings

The history and development of buildings is a fascinating area for model makers. There is an abundance of ideal pictorial reference material available in the form of postcards, periodicals, posters and books – children's library books are particularly useful as their illustrations and accompanying text tend to be simple, clear and concise.

Making a 3-D model from a photograph or picture can be as simple or as complex as you wish to make it. Unless you are wanting to produce a perfectly scaled model, probably the most important aspect is to try to keep things in proportion – windows, doors, chimneys, steps, fences. Having gathered enough comprehensive reference material, draw the building on to paper, breaking it down through several quick sketches into simple structural shapes (you do not need to be an artist to do this), then start the basic construction. Although some

parts of the model might be completed in one go, it may take several attempts to get another part right – so have plenty of practice-paper to hand (used photocopy paper is ideal). Build a complete prototype with practice-paper before embarking on the final model. All structural and design problems should be resolved at this stage, but you will need to test samples of the final paper or card for strength and to see how it cuts, bends and creases. You will also need to experiment with different media for brick, stone, plaster, wood and other effects.

Model making can be as easy or as complex as you wish to make it. These windmills are based on sketches from a children's library book.

Materials and equipment

Most of the following list can be used as a basis for general model-making requirements. To make the wooden windmill you will need an A3 (12 x 16½ in) sheet of thin card; thicker card for the steps (small strips of this will also be attached to the sails); felt-tipped markers or coloured pencils to create the wood and stone effects; a brass paper-stud; sticky tape; double-sided sticky tape (DSST); scissors; craft knife; steel-edged rule; cutting board; measuring rule; tracing paper and pencil. I used buff-coloured card for the wooden sections but white card 'coloured in' will do just as well.

1. Trace six tower sections on to the card. Pencil the door and window areas on to one section, filling them in with black or dark brown. Colour the sections to resemble thin planks of wood then cut them out using the knife and steel-edged rule. Score lightly along the dotted lines.

3. Stick a strip of DSST to the right-hand flap of each tower section. Stick all the sections together. Cut out the hexagonal tower top and secure it to the top of the tower sections with small pieces of sticky tape.

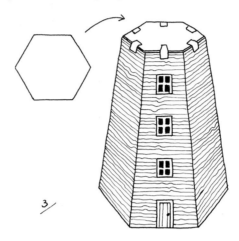

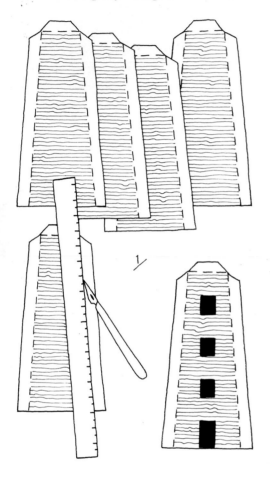

4. Lightly score the curved dotted lines on the two cap sides. Colour the sides and the cap roof to resemble narrow planks of wood then cut them out. Using the knife, cut a small vertical slit in one of the cap sides, as marked on the diagram. Bend the flaps backwards.

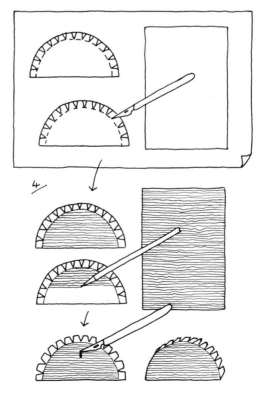

2. Using the knife, carefully cut out the windows and door. Stick a piece of DSST on the back of each and position over the dark areas.

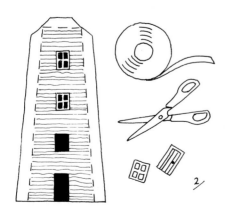

Key to diagram on page 19
1. Cap roof
2. Cap side (cut 2)
3. Tower section (cut 6)
4. Tower top
5. Base section (cut 6)
6. Sail (cut 2)
7. Thin sail bar (cut 4)
8. Thick sail bar (cut 4)
9. Steps
10. Door
11. Window (cut 3)

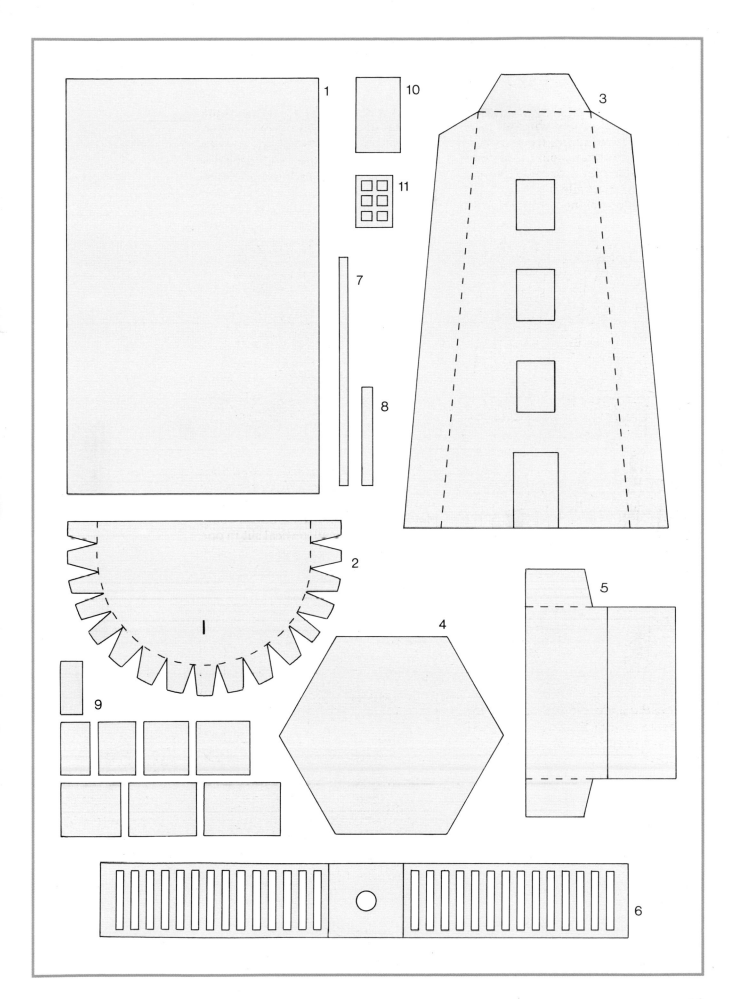

1

10

11

3

7

8

2

9

4

5

6

5. Turn the large section over and stick strips of DSST along the edges, as shown. Attach the end pieces to the large section, carefully bending the card round.

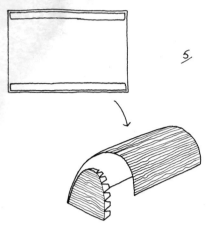

7. Push the brass stud through the sails, then through the slit in the cap. Open the prongs at the back, making sure that the sails are free to spin. Stick a strip of DSST to the top of the tower, as shown. Stick another strip to the opposite side. Firmly attach the top to the tower – position it so that the sails do not touch the tower as they spin.

6. Carefully cut out and colour the two sails. Make the central hole with the knife or a hole punch. Stick the two sails together using DSST. Cut out, colour and attach the four thin sail bars; position them as shown on the photograph (see page 17). Cut four thick sail bars from the thicker card, colour and attach to the sails as shown below. (If you blow like crazy these will help the sails to spin.)

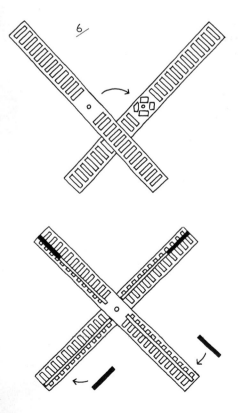

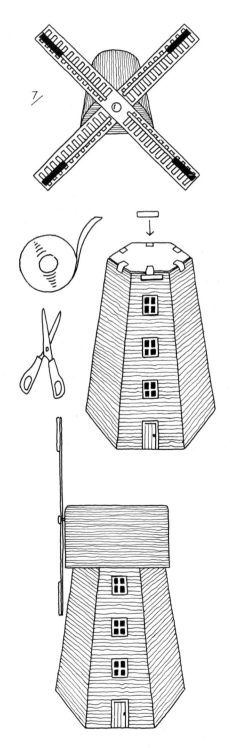

8. Cut out the six base sections. Lightly score along the dotted lines, then colour the card to resemble stones. Attach a strip of DSST to the right-hand flap of each section, then stick them all together.

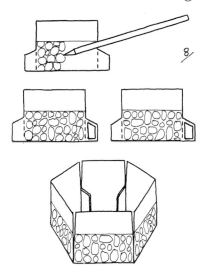

10. The depth of each step should be slightly more than 2mm ($^1/_{16}$in). To achieve this, stick pieces of card together using DSST. When the depth is reached, cut out and stick each step together. Colour the steps then attach them to the base, directly under the door, using a piece of DSST.

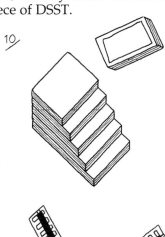

9. Push the base into the tower. The flaps joining the tower section should slide easily through the slits in the base and stop where the base flaps start. Secure the base from the inside with pieces of sticky tape, as shown.

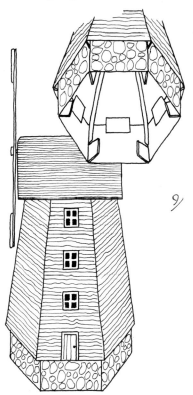

simple
origami

Simple origami

The ancient art of folding paper is believed to have been developed in Japan, though it may well have started with the invention of paper by the Chinese, during the second century AD. The word origami comes from two Japanese words, the verb 'ori' (to fold) and the noun 'kami' (paper).

Strictly speaking, origami is the art of *folding* paper and does not include cutting, gluing or stapling. The following examples are easy to construct and comply with the 'fold only' rule (apart from a small piece of sticky tape on one of the bracelets and florist's wire to support the flower heads!). Accuracy and precision are most important for successful paper folding. If a square piece of paper is required, it must be perfectly square.

The paper should have the ability to hold a crease; for example, paper towels, tissue paper, newspaper and paper tissues are all inappropriate. Papers with a very shiny surface or those coated with a coloured pigment are also unsuitable. Most art and craft shops have a wide range of papers which can be used, including pastel paper, thin white or tinted watercolour paper, cartridge paper, paper with a different colour on the front and reverse side, textured paper and patterned gift-wrap paper. Try experimenting with thin wallpaper or apply a simple pattern using coloured pencils or felt-tipped pens to tinted cartridge paper.

Generally speaking, the more complex the piece of origami, the easier it is to work with thinner paper. The thing to remember is that the colour, texture or pattern of the paper should not dominate the structural creases. Always practise with cheaper paper before embarking on the final piece. Computer, photocopy and typing paper are ideal for first attempts. If these are unavailable, try using newspaper, old wrapping paper or magazine pages.

Folds

The two basic folds used in origami are
A, the valley fold, and B, the peak fold.

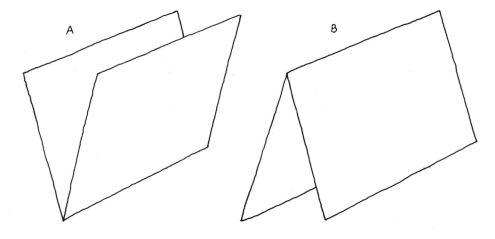

Origami has become a very popular, world-wide art form. A great deal of satisfaction can be gained from achieving completion of the first attempted model.

Butterfly

For this model I used yellow typing paper. At stage one, after folding the square in half diagonally, I laid a paper doily over the triangle and coloured through the holes with a spirit-based felt-tipped marker.

1. Cut a 125mm (5in) square. Make a valley fold, taking corner D to corner B.

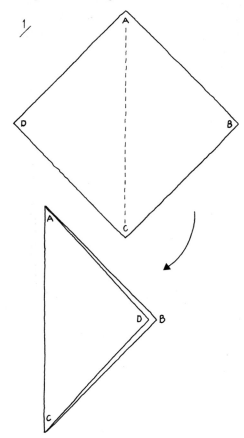

2. Make a peak fold, taking corner A to corner C.

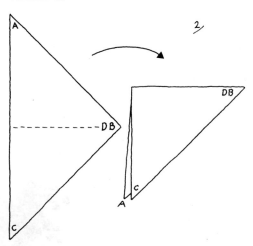

3. Make a valley fold with the top layer only, taking corner C to corner DB. Turn the model over and repeat, taking corner A to corner CDB.

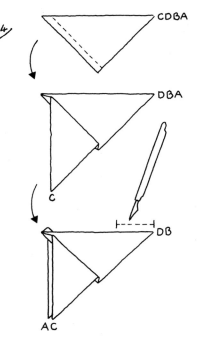

4. Make a peak fold 6mm (¼in) from the edge, bringing corner C down. Turn the model over and repeat with corner A. Cut the peak fold from corner DB to a length of 25mm (1in).

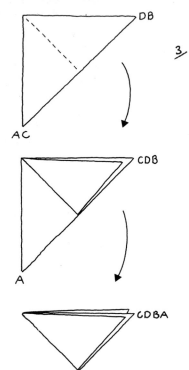

5. Make a valley fold along the dotted line, on the top layer only (from the end of the slit made in step 4), bringing corner A upwards. Turn the paper over and repeat with corner C.

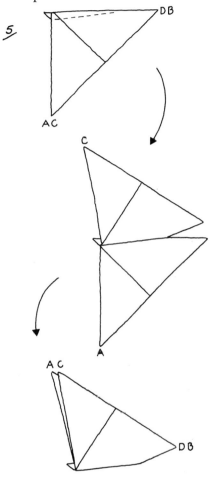

6. Make a valley fold (along the dotted line shown below) in the two wing tips, then open out the wings.

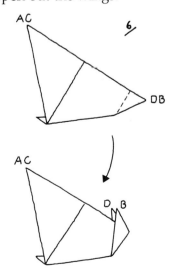

Hydrangea

To make one hydrangea you will need fifteen lengths of fine florist's wire, each approximately 180mm (7in) long (the wire can easily be cut with a pair of old scissors); a roll of green florist's tape; small strips of yellow crepe paper for the stamens; fifteen 60mm (2³/₈in) squares of paper – these can be one colour or varying shades of the same colour. For the hydrangeas in the photograph (see page 25) I used combinations of coloured photocopy paper and thin cartridge paper.

1. Make valley folds four times, unfolding the square after each crease. Remake fold A–B to form a triangle.

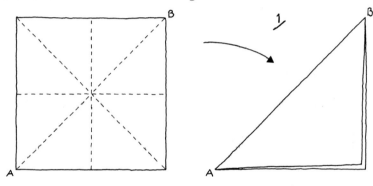

2. Open corner A, push it into the centre and press the two outer corners together. Repeat with corner B.

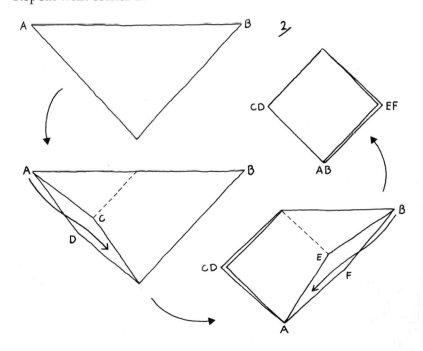

27

3. Working with the top layer first, fold as indicated so that C and E touch the centre crease. Turn over and repeat with D and F.

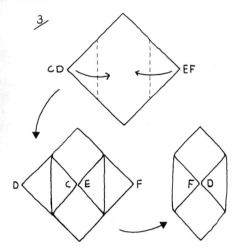

4. Turn the model upside down to position the loose corners at the top. Valley-fold the top layer as indicated, bringing the edges together in the centre. Repeat with the reverse side.

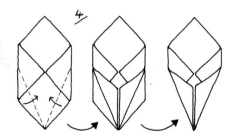

5. Make a valley fold, creasing as sharply as possible, horizontally through the centre. Unfold, then carefully open out the petals. This is one floret. Repeat with the other fourteen squares (more if you want a fuller flower head).

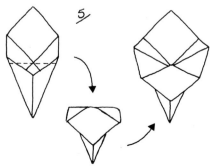

6. Bend the top of each piece of wire to form a little hook. Take a small strip of yellow crepe paper, roughly 10 x 75mm ($^3/_8$ x 3in), and push one end through the hook. Wrap it round to form a tight point at the top. Cut the tip off.

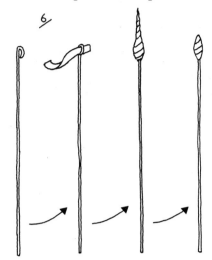

7. Push the sharp end of the wire carefully through the centre of the floret, then pull it through until only half of the stamen is visible as shown below.

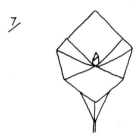

8. Take a piece of florist's tape approximately 150mm (6in) long. Tuck one end into the back of the floret and wind the tape securely round the floret base, then tightly down to cover half the wire.

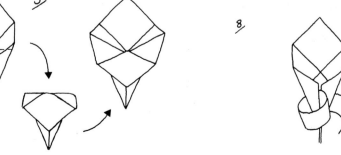

9. Repeat with the remaining wires. Bring all the florets together to form a neat bunch. Wrap a length of florist's tape round them all to make one stem.

10. The leaves are made separately, in two shades of green. They vary in length from 150 to 200mm (6 to 8in). Take a strip of paper 40mm (1½in) wide. Fold it in half lengthways and draw the leaf and stem as shown. Cut the shape out and open it up. Some of the leaves can be creased backwards, as shown.

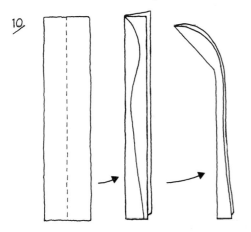

Vase

1. Using a piece of paper 255mm (10in) square, make four valley folds as shown. Unfold after each crease, then refold to form a rectangle.

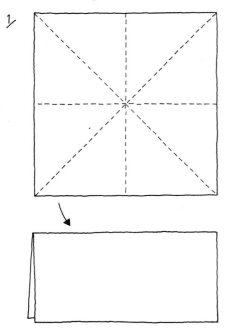

2. Open the left side, push corner A to the bottom edge, then fold corner B back to corner C. Repeat with the right side to form a triangle.

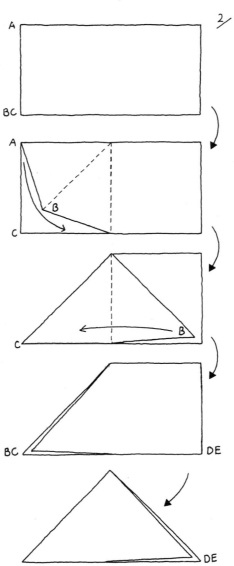

3. Turn the paper round and with the open edges upwards make a pencil mark 45mm (1¾in) from the centre point along the angled edge and another on the top edge 28mm (1⅛in) from the centre crease. Valley-fold as indicated.

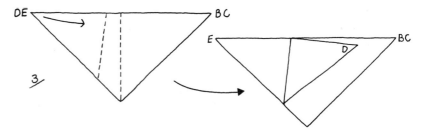

This delicate but strong place mat made from Chinese paper is pretty enough to be used as a candle base or Christmas decoration.

4. Valley-fold this section in half, then tuck corner D down inside, as shown.

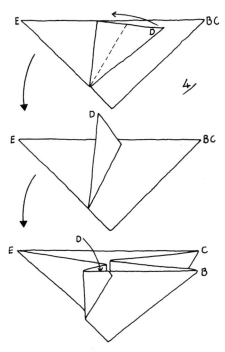

5. Repeat with corner B, then turn over and repeat again with corners C and E.

6. Make a sharp valley fold at the base, as shown, then unfold. Very carefully open out the vase, pushing the base into a square.

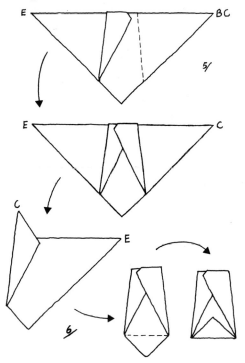

Place mat

This pretty mat is made from two patterned Chinese papers which have a texture rather like fine fabric, but any thin paper would be appropriate. The final piece can also be used as a Christmas tree decoration or the base for a candle. Larger or smaller versions can be made by altering the size of the segments.

To make a mat similar to the one in the photograph you will need forty-two rectangles, the sides of which must be in the ratio 2:3. For this exercise I am using rectangles measuring 80 x 120mm (3 x 4½in). The effect is certainly more interesting if you use two complementary papers – in which case you will need twenty-one of each.

1. With right side of the paper facing down, valley-fold the top third, then peak-fold the lower third.

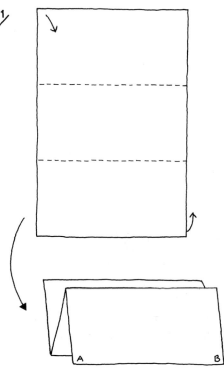

2. Valley-fold corners A and B, as shown.

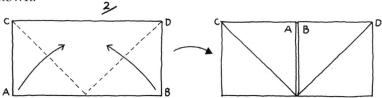

3. Turn the segment over and valley-fold corners C and D. Turn the segment over again and gently pull point Z out so that corners X and Y come together. Crease all the sides firmly. This is one segment. Repeat the process with the remaining rectangles.

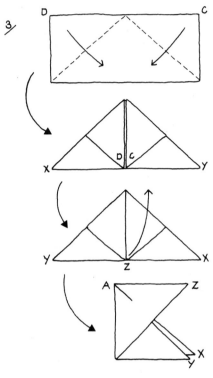

4. To join the segments together, slide the second colour into the first, as shown. Push the lower point A in so that the upper part splays out like a fan. Tuck flap Y into the second segment and repeat with the back flap X.

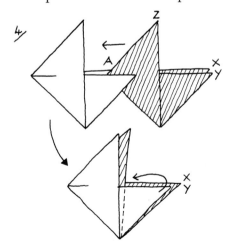

5. Continue interlocking the segments until the whole circle is complete, sliding the last segment into the first, as before.

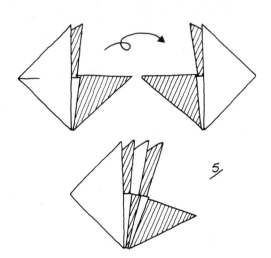

6. To make a candle base, cut a circle of card and attach it to the bottom of a candle using a flat drawing pin. Slip the mat over the candle. Cut a small circle of clear cellophane to go over the mat. This will protect it from drips of wax.

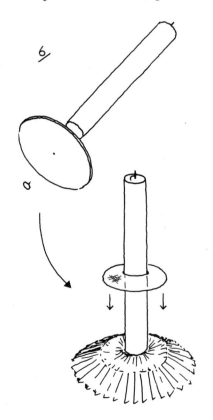

Trinket box

1. Using a 180mm (7in) square piece of paper (I used gift wrap for the example in the photograph) and with the patterned side facing up, make valley folds horizontally and vertically, unfolding after each crease.

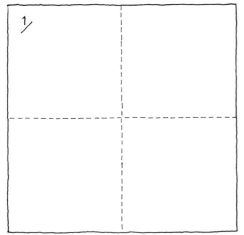

2. Turn the paper over and bring each corner to the centre, making sharp creases along the edges.

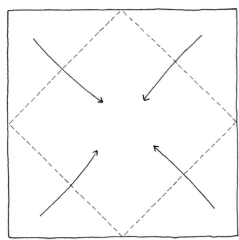

3. Valley-fold two opposite sides into the centre, make sharp creases, then unfold. Repeat with the other two sides, then unfold. The central square will form the base of the box.

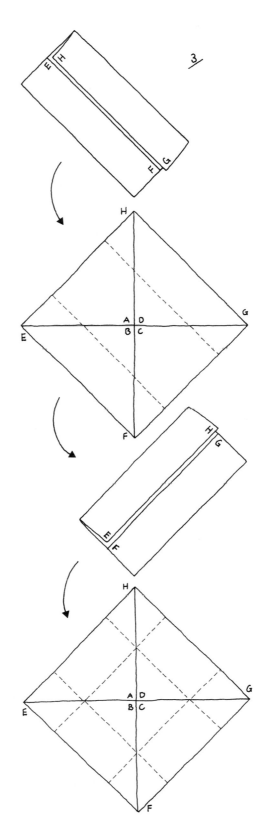

4. Open out corners B and D, as shown. Lift corner B up, together with the two sides marked S, so that corners E and F come to the centre point and the two Zs and two Ys meet.

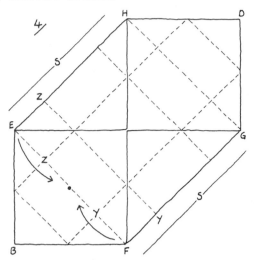

5. Fold the flap neatly over so that corner B meets A and C in the middle.

6. Repeat with the opposite side, bringing corners H and G to the centre point. Fold the flap over as before.

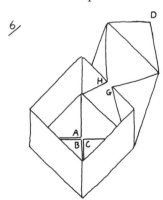

Bracelet

The gold lining from a chocolate box and striped wrapping paper were used to make the metallic bracelet. You will need approximately thirty strips of paper (depending on the size of your hand) the sides of which are in the ratio 1:8. Strips measuring 10 x 80mm ($^3/_8$ x 3in) were used to make the bracelet shown in the photograph on page 25. The same paper can be used throughout or different combinations of colours and patterns.

1. With the patterned side face down, fold one of the strips in half. Unfold, then fold sides A and B inwards, leaving a small gap at the centre crease.

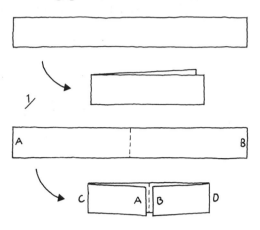

2. Fold in half so that C and D come together. Repeat this procedure with all the strips.

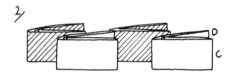

3. Carefully push the second segment into the first, then pull it down as far as it will go. You may need to trim the long edge slightly to get a good fit.

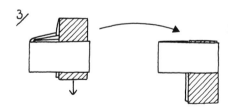

4. Push the next segment in horizontally, as shown. Push the next one in vertically and so on, until the chain is complete.

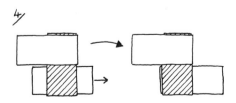

5. To join the bracelet unfold the last unused strip once, as shown. Push it

into the last segment, bring the first one round and slide it between the unfolded strip. Tuck the ends down inside.

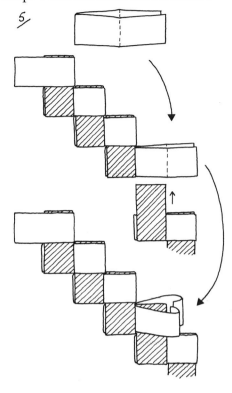

Woven bracelet

This was made using a strip of silver wrapping paper. It had a plain white underside which I coloured blue with a felt-tipped marker. In order to achieve the woven effect the paper really needs to have contrasting sides. The woven strip can be as wide or as long as you wish. A wider version makes a good book mark.

1. Take a long strip of paper, for example the length of a sheet of wrapping paper, 10mm (³/₈in) wide. Fold it in half to form a 90° angle.

2. Valley-fold the left side over.

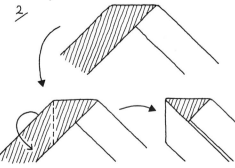

3. Peak-fold the right side and bring it over the left side, as shown.

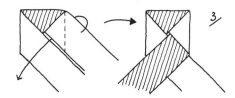

4. Valley-fold the left side, as shown, then peak-fold the right side as before. Continue until the required length is reached.

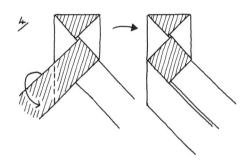

5. To join the bracelet, cut the left and right strips as shown. Lift and tuck the strip into the full section. Bring the bracelet round and attach a piece of DSST to the top sections, as shown. Slide the cut strip into the gap and press firmly together.

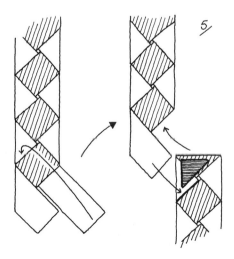

6. If you are making a book mark, finish the bottom edge by cutting the strips along the dotted lines (right) then tuck the end into the gap. A piece of DSST will help to secure the end.

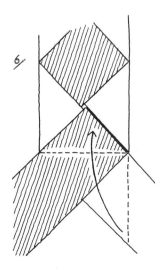

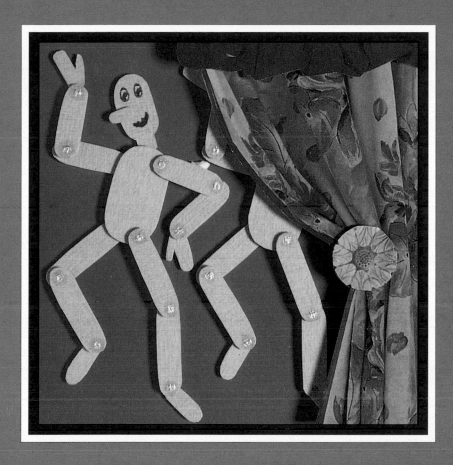

puppets
and dolls

Finger puppets

The complete set of puppets opposite would make an ideal gift for the small child who loves a bedtime story. They are made from good-quality coloured cartridge paper. The basic body shape is the same throughout: a half-circle folded round to form a cone. Various ears, eyes, snouts and tails are then attached to give each puppet its individual animal character.

I have used a combination of double-sided sticky tape (DSST) and liquid PVA glue because in some instances, one is easier to use than the other. It is wise to experiment with a few pieces of paper before starting. When using the PVA you will need to hold the surfaces together for a few seconds until the glue sets.

The diagrams on pages 40 and 43 can be traced on to the cartridge. Lay the tracing paper over the diagram and trace in the usual way. Turn the tracing over, tape it lightly on to the cartridge and then draw over the same lines – this is less messy than scribbling over the back of the tracing paper.

Use a craft knife and steel-edged ruler to cut the straight lines, and scissors for the curves and circles. Practise using them before starting on the real thing.

Short broken lines on the diagrams indicate a score line. To do this, simply run the back of your craft knife lightly along the line, using the ruler as a guide. The paper will then bend cleanly. Where the broken lines are curved, you will have to use the knife free-hand. Again, do some practising before attempting the actual puppet.

Do not bother tracing all the lines on pieces b2, b3, b4, b7 and d6. These merely indicate that the pieces need a fringe-like cut. Use your knife and try to cut free-hand, making the fringe as fine as possible.

To curl the whiskers hold a whisker in one hand and with the other, pull the blunt edge of the scissors along, as if peeling a carrot. Do not pull too hard. Practise with some strips of paper; you will soon learn how much pressure is required. The more firmly the edge is held against the paper, the tighter the curl will be. Use the same technique for curling tails and the lion's mane.

When the puppet is complete, stick a small square of DSST on the front inside of the cone. This will stick to the finger and prevent the puppet from wobbling. Though the completed puppets are quite sturdy, they are rather too large for little fingers, so I recommend adult use only!

The display stand can also be made from coloured cartridge, or a slightly stiffer card. The instructions and diagram are on page 46 and 47.

Materials and equipment

Coloured cartridge papers; tracing paper; a well-sharpened 2H pencil; craft knife and blades; steel-edged ruler; small pair of sharp, pointed scissors; double-sided sticky tape (DSST); liquid PVA glue; a fine black felt-tipped pen for drawing eyes, noses, mouths and hair follicles. You will need a large sheet of thick cartridge paper or thin board that measures at least 550 x 800mm (22 x 32in), if you intend to make the display stand.

The complete set of finger puppets on their own display stand (from left to right):
Top row
Lion, owl and rabbit.
Middle row
Elephant, panda and crocodile.
Bottom row
Cockerel, mouse and pig.

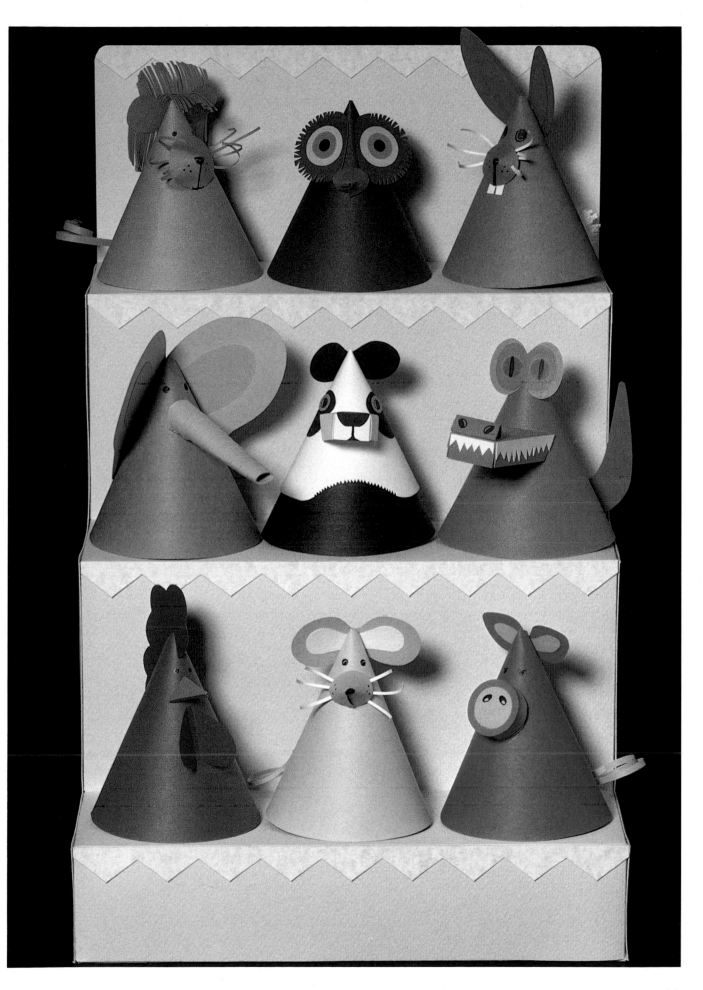

39

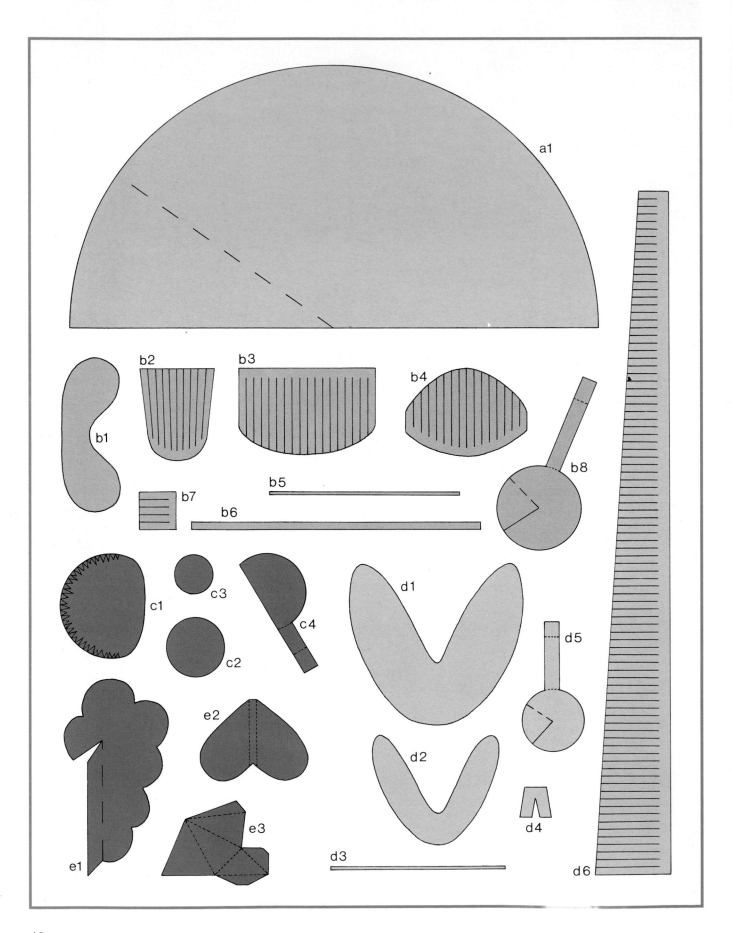

The basic body shape

Please read the introduction on page 38 before starting.

Fold the main body of the puppet (a1) round to form a cone, using two strips of DSST to secure.

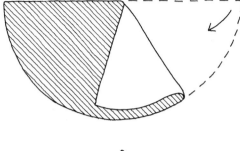

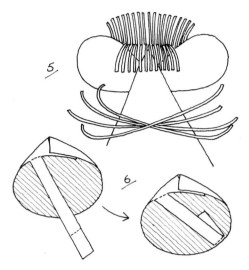

7. Curl the tail (b6), then stick the fringe (b7) round the end. Attach completed tail to the back of the body.

8. Draw two dots for the eyes.

The lion

1. Make the main body as shown above.

2. Curl the fringe (b2) slightly and attach to the back of the ears (b1).

3. Curl the mane (b3) even less slightly and attach across the back of the ears.

4. Curl the other piece of the mane (b4) slightly, attach it as shown and then stick the complete piece to the body.

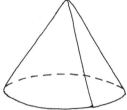

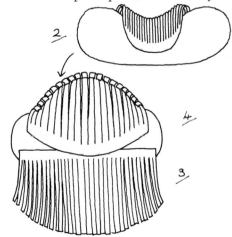

5. Curl whiskers and stick as shown.

6. Form the snout (b8) into a flattish cone. Bend and stick the flap. Draw the nose, mouth and hair follicles and then position the snout over the whiskers.

The owl

1. Make the main body as shown above.

2. Using your knife, make small cuts from the outer edges of c1 to indicate feathers.

3. Draw a nice round eye on each inner eye piece (c3), stick on to the outer eye (c2), and then on to the eye feathers (c1).

4. Fold and stick the beak (c4) to form a cone. Bend and stick the flap, as shown.

5. Position the completed eyes and beak as shown in the photograph on page 39.

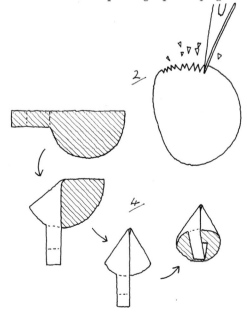

Key to diagram on page 40

General
a1. Body of all puppets

The lion
b1. Ears
b2. Fringe
b3. Part of mane
b4. Part of mane
b5. Whiskers (cut 4)
b6. Tail
b7. Fringe for tail
b8. Snout

The owl
c1. Eye feathers (cut 2)
c2. Outer eyes (cut 2)
c3. Inner eyes (cut 2)
c4. Beak

The rabbit
d1. Outer ears
d2. Inner ears
d3. Whiskers (cut 3)
d4. Teeth
d5. Snout
d6. Tail

The cockerel
e1. Comb
e2. Wattle
e3. Beak

The rabbit

1. Make the main body of the rabbit as shown on page 41.

2. Stick the inner ears (d2) to the outer ears (d1), then attach to the body.

3. Curl the whiskers (d3) and then position as shown in the illustration.

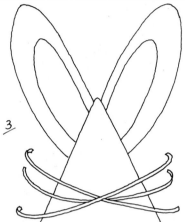

4. Fold and stick the snout (d5) into a flattish cone. Bend and stick the flap as shown. Draw the nose and hair follicles.

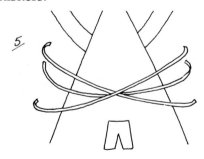

5. Stick the teeth (d4) below the whiskers.

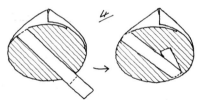

6. Position the completed snout over the whiskers and the top of the teeth, then draw in the eyes, as shown.

7. Fringe the tail (d6), roll up tightly and secure the end with a small piece of DSST. Attach to body with more DSST.

The cockerel

1. Make the main body of the cockerel as shown on page 41.

2. Cut a slit down the back of the body, long enough to fit the flap of the comb (e1): the flap is indicated by broken lines on the diagram below. Carefully push the flap in.

3. Draw two dots for the eyes.

4. Fold and stick the beak (e3) as shown. Stick it to the body, just below the eyes.

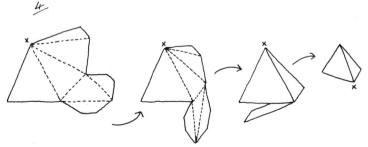

5. Fold the wattle (e2) and position it underneath the beak.

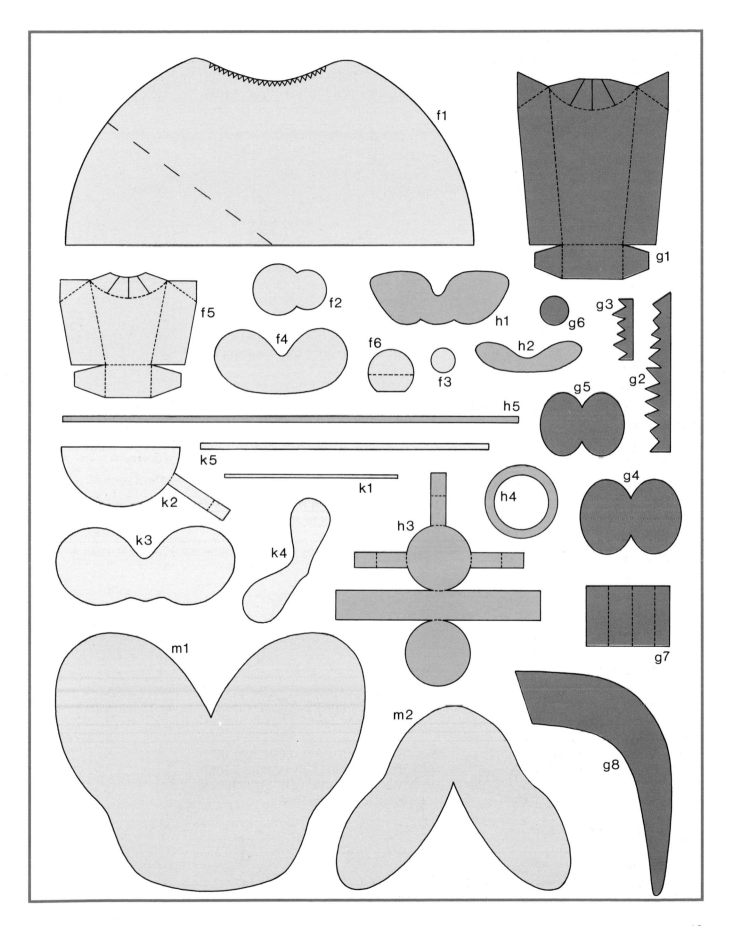

The panda

1. Make the main body of the panda as shown on page 41.

2. Using your knife, take small cuts from the white body piece (f1) and fold to make a cone. Put dabs of glue inside then slide on top of the main body.

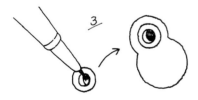

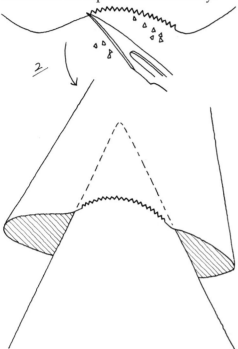

3. Draw eyes on the inner eye (f3) then stick on to the black outer eye piece (f2).

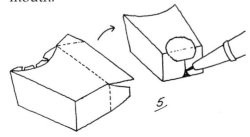

4. Attach the ears.

5. Fold and stick the snout (f5) as shown. Stick on the nose (f6) and draw in the mouth.

6. Position the completed snout just below the eyes.

The crocodile

1. Make the main body of the crocodile as shown on page 41.

2. Fold and stick the mouthpiece (g1).

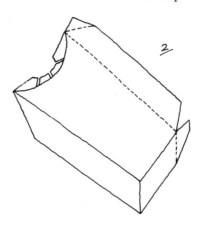

3. Carefully stick the side and front teeth (g2 and g3) on to the mouthpiece.

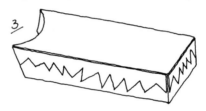

4. Fold and stick the snout (g7). Draw in the nostrils. Stick the snout on to the mouthpiece, then position the mouthpiece on the body.

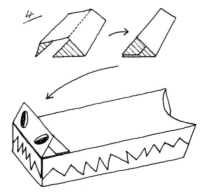

5. Draw 'slit' eyes on centre eye (g6). Stick these on to the inner eye (g5), then on to the outer eye (g4). Attach the completed eyes to the body.

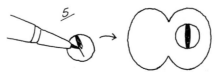

6. Position the tail at the back.

The pig

1. Make the main body of the pig as shown on page 41.

2. Stick the inner ears (h2) to the outer ears (h1), then attach to the body.

3. Draw two dots for the eyes.

4. Fold and stick the snout (h3).

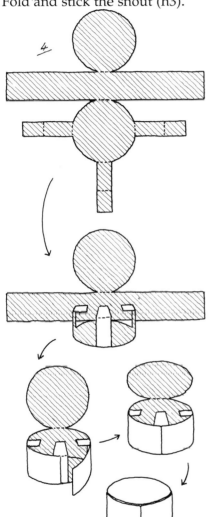

5. Carefully stick ring (h4) round the edge of the snout. Draw in the nostrils.

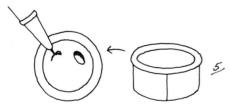

6. Position the snout below the eyes.

7. Curl the tail (h5) using maximum pressure, to make a very curly tail, and then attach it to the back of the body.

The mouse

1. Make the main body of the mouse as shown on page 41.

2. Stick the inner ears (k4) to the outer ears (k3), then attach both to the body, bowing them slightly.

3. Draw in two eyes on the body.

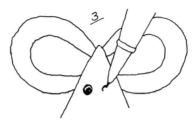

4. Curl and position the whiskers (k1).

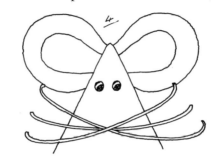

5. Fold and stick the snout (k2) to form a cone. Bend and stick the flap.

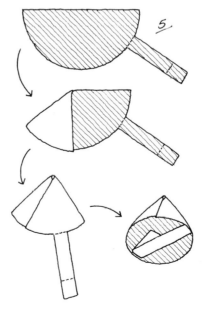

6. Draw a nose and hair follicles, then attach the snout over the whiskers.

7. Curl the tail (k5) lightly and attach it to the back of the body.

The elephant

1. Make the main body of the elephant as shown on page 41.

2. Cut a 10 x 400mm (³/₈ x 16in) strip of cartridge paper. Fold the end tightly round a thin knitting needle or similar object). Continue to wind the strip round the needle, then secure the end with a dab of glue.

3. Gently pull the strip out to form a tube. Flatten it slightly at the narrow end. Carefully cut the wide end so that it will lie flat against the body, leaving a small flap.

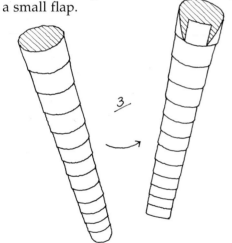

4. Cut a slit for the trunk, as shown. Put a dab of glue above the slit, then push the trunk flap in.

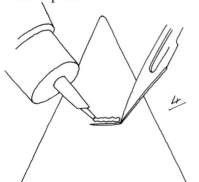

5. Stick the inner ears to the outer ears, then attach to the body.

6. Draw two dots for the eyes.

The display stand

This can be made from coloured cartridge, but thin card will prove more stable. As the structure is rather large the diagram opposite has been reduced. However, I hope that the inclusion of relevant dimensions will help you to construct it.

Short broken lines indicate light scoring on the top surface of the paper. The longer broken lines (marked with an x) indicate light scoring on the underside, thus a step is formed. Use strips of DSST on the flaps when assembling the stand.

1. Secure the base to the stepped sides first, then carefully bend and crease the steps, bringing them down, one by one, and attaching them to the sides.

2. Attach the decorative pieces to the top of each step and to the back piece.

3. Attach the back piece to the rear of the top step.

Note The proportions of your stand will be a little different from those of the one in the photograph, which had to be changed slightly to accommodate the page size.

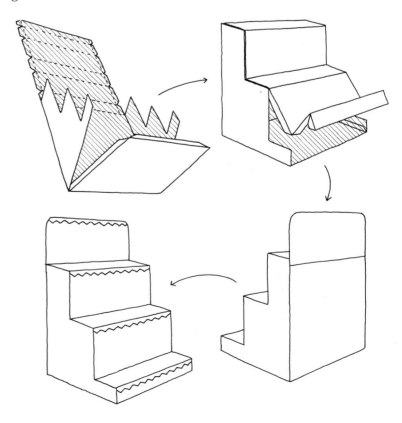

This pattern for the display stand must be enlarged on a photocopier, or redrawn to the dimensions given.

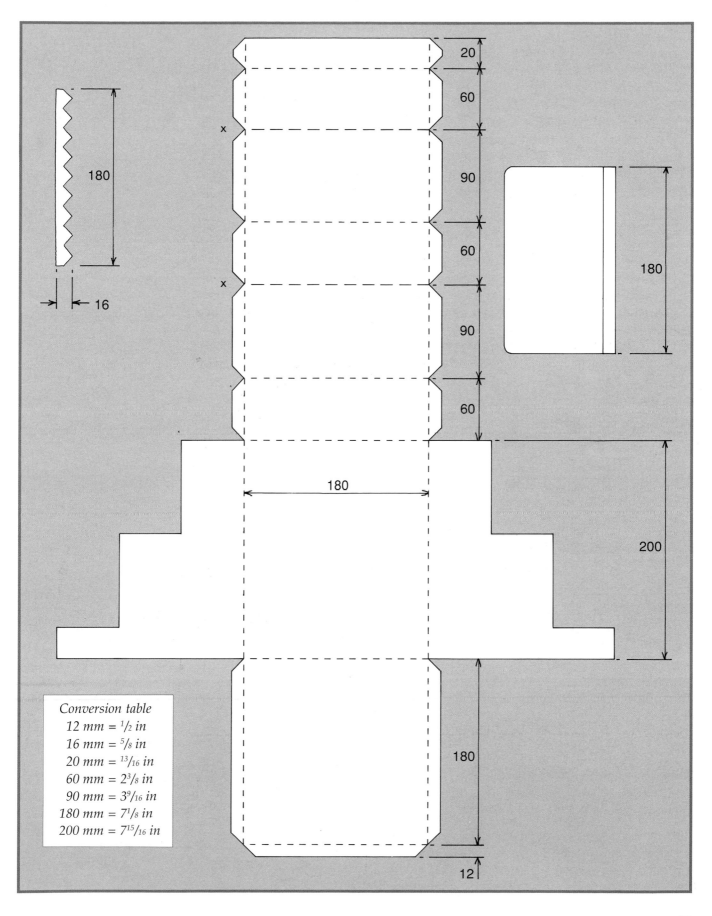

20

60

x

90

60

x

90

60

180

180

180

16

200

180

12

Conversion table
12 mm = 1/2 in
16 mm = 5/8 in
20 mm = 13/16 in
60 mm = 2 3/8 in
90 mm = 3 9/16 in
180 mm = 7 1/8 in
200 mm = 7 15/16 in

Dressed dolls

Here are some simple dolls to be dressed. They have plump little arms and legs and no trace of voluptuous lips, golden tresses or macho jaws. There are six outfits – a chef's uniform, clown's attire, nightwear, a spacesuit, beachwear and a DIY outfit. All are male and female interchangeable apart from the nightwear.

When designing your own outfits, it is more practical to make all-in-one suits which hang easily from the shoulders. Skirts and trousers which attach at the hips tend to fall off. If a short skirt is wanted, cut the skirt (with shoulder straps), tights and shoes from one piece of card, then add a separate top and any suitable accessories. Additional bits and pieces can be placed in pockets or, like the hot-water bottle, can appear to be held in the hand. Pocket contents can, if wished, be secured permanently by sticking a small piece of double-sided sticky tape (DSST) at the back. Hats are simply held on to the head using the traditional bent flap or a separate piece of card stuck to the back of the hat. The clothes are coloured with felt-tipped pens. The secret of making them look three-dimensional is to use one or two shades of grey, on the seams and fabric folds, at the waist, down openings like the dressing-gown front, and round collars and cuffs.

The dolls and outfits are made from thin white card. Before tracing and cutting out the dolls, stick a piece of flesh-coloured paper on to the card, using a thin film of Cow Gum. This is better than using felt-tipped pens because it gives a flatter finish to the colour.

I find it easier to cut out with a knife because scissors tend to bend the card. Using the knife will produce a clean edge and a slightly ridged, crumpled edge

Any number of outfits can be made for these simple cut-out dolls. Pockets for 'tools of the trade' add interest and the clothes are less likely to fall off because they are all hung from the shoulders. See also page 50.

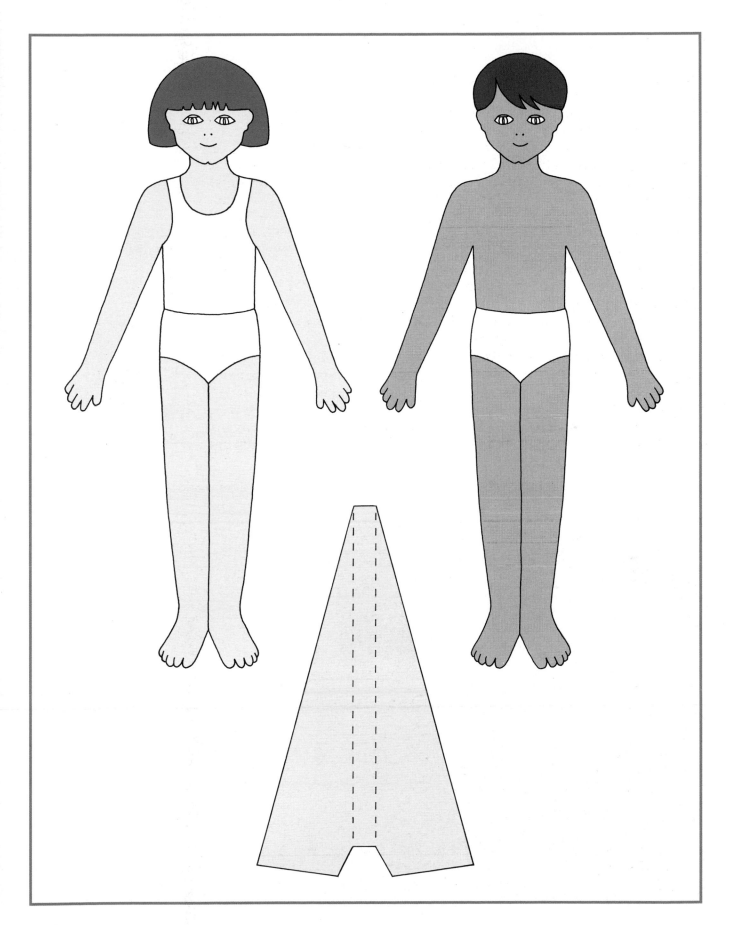

either side of the cut. Make sure the crumpled edge is on the piece of card to be discarded. Practise beforehand. When cutting intricate pieces such as fingers, chip carefully away at the card, rather than trying to cut round in one go.

When the items of clothing with pockets have been cut out and coloured, cut a narrow slit in the top of the pocket, as shown in the drawing for the chef's outfit. The item can be secured at the back with a piece of sticky tape, if it is to remain permanently in the pocket.

Some of the hats, and the hot-water bottle, are clipped on to the doll using a small piece of card, half of which is stuck to the item with a smaller piece of DSST, as shown in each drawing.

The back supports for the dolls are made from stiff black cartridge, which is less obtrusive than the white card. Lightly score along the dotted lines, using the back of the knife and a steel-edged ruler, then attach it to the back of the doll with a thin strip of DSST.

For the budding couturier there is a set of mannequin dolls on pages 54 to 57. Clothes for these can be originally designed or inspired by the latest collections.

Materials and equipment

Thin white card for the dolls and outfits; stiff black cartridge for the support stands; flesh-coloured papers for the dolls; coloured felt-tipped pens, including greys; sharp craft knife; scissors; steel-edged ruler; gold poster paint and gold foil (from sweet wrappers) for the spacesuit and the clown's boots; silver paper for the tie; silver poster paint for the hammer and paintbrush; adhesive tape; double-sided sticky tape; Cow Gum; a cutting mat or piece of thick card.

Key to diagram on page 51

The spacesuit
a1. *Suit*
a2. *Helmet*
a3. *Elbow bands*
a4. *Shoulder bands*
a5. *Waist band*
a6. *Knee bands*
a7. *Instrument pack*

The chef's outfit
b1. *Uniform*
b2. *Hat*
b3. *Rolling pin*
b4. *Whisk*

The clown's outfit
c1. *Shirt*
c2. *Trousers*
c3. *Tie*
c4. *Face and hat*

Chef's outfit

This one-piece suit is made to look like a separate top and trousers simply by drawing a thick line of grey across the top of the trousers. Shading is also applied to the shoes, just below the trousers. The utensils are inserted into the slit in the top of the pocket and can be secured at the back, if wished.

Position the small piece of card for the hat as shown below.

Spacesuit

After cutting out and colouring all the pieces, scrunch the gold paper up then press it flat. Stick the paper to the suit with a thin film of Cow Gum on each surface. Lay the suit, gold side down, on to a cutting mat and cut away excess paper. Turn the suit over and carefully cut the paper away from the boots and gloves. Stick the extra pieces on to the suit as shown below.

Position a small piece of card for the helmet as shown for the chef's outfit.

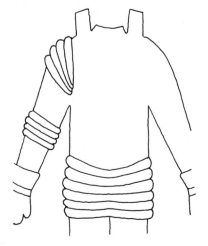

Clown's outfit

After colouring all the pieces, scrunch the silver paper up then flatten it. Apply a thin film of Cow Gum to the tie and the back of the silver paper, then stick together. Lay the tie, silver side down, and cut away the excess paper.

Use the same method for the gold boots. Separate the boots by indenting a line using the end of the knife handle. Repeat for the laces. For clarity of colour I used adhesive dots on the trousers and flower centre. Position a small piece of card for the clown's head as shown for the chef's outfit.

Beachwear

After cutting out and colouring all the pieces, cut a slit in the bucket and insert the spade. The bucket will stay in position when the handle is slipped over the hand. Add plenty of grey shading to the peak of the hat to give the appearance of bending upwards.

Nightwear

After cutting out and colouring all the pieces, cut a slit in the top of the pocket of the dressing gown for the teddy. Position the piece of card for the hot-water bottle as shown below.

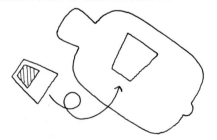

DIY outfit

After colouring all the pieces, cut a slit in each pocket and insert the hammer and paintbrush. Apply grey shading to the shoes, just below the trousers. Bend the peak of the hat slightly upwards.

Key to diagram on page 53

The DIY outfit
d1. Shirt
d2. Dungarees
d3. Hat
d4. Hammer
d5. Paintbrush

Nightwear
e1. Nightdress
e2. Dressing gown
e3. Teddy bear
e4. Hot-water bottle

Beachwear
f1. Shirt and shorts
f2. Hat
f3. Spade
f4. Bucket

Mannequin dolls can be used to plan a co-ordinated wardrobe. New ideas for designs can be taken from current fashion magazines or historical fashion books borrowed from the library.

Mannequins

The general instructions for making the mannequins, shown in the photograph opposite, are exactly as for the dolls in the previous section, but a little more time has been taken to produce fabric textures and prints.

Ideas for more clothes can be taken from current fashion magazines, historical fashion books, window displays or television fashion programmes. An entire wardrobe of co-ordinating garments could be produced for each of the seasons; for holidaying in hot or cold climates; for a wedding trousseau; or simply for a collection of mix-and-match clothes to wear at work or home.

The interest comes in discovering different methods of producing a realistic print or weave. I have used felt-tipped markers throughout, but coloured watercolour pencils, wax crayons, charcoal, chalk and pastels can also be used. Water-based paints are tricky because as the paint dries it distorts the card, though dry brush painting (using a minimum amount of water) can give interesting results.

A 3-D effect is achieved by using layers of grey – this is clearly seen on the left mannequin opposite, on the lemon skirt and white stockings. Hints on how to obtain the pink dots and green stripes on the other two outfits and for fake animal skin and checks are given on page 58.

Lemon and grey outfit

Only a suggestion of colour is used to achieve the appearance of soft, fine fabric, as in this off-the-shoulder blouse. The skirt fabric appears heavier because solid colour has been applied.

The clutch bag does not need additional card at the back; it is simply slipped between the fingers and thumb and held in position by the skirt.

Blue and pink outfit

This is a straightforward one-piece trouser suit with a separate top which could be fabric, suède or leather. A leather garment hangs more stiffly than fabric, so cut and colour the piece accordingly – study photographs and sketches in magazines. The hat is secured using a piece of card, as shown in the drawing.

Green outfit

I have not made separate footwear because little shoes, boots or sandals can get lost and soon become scruffy. It is therefore necessary to have a felt-tipped marker the same colour as the flesh-coloured paper used for the whole mannequin, as on the legs of this model.

The lining for the hood is attached to one side of the back (as shown in the drawing) so that the head can slide in sideways.

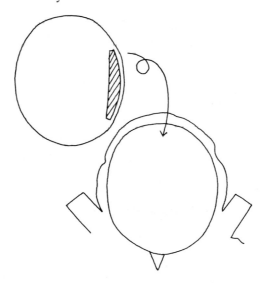

The shoulder-bag is secured in position by a small piece of card attached to the back of the mannequin.

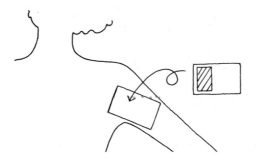

Key to diagram on pages 56 and 57

General
a1. Mannequin
a2. Back support

Lemon and grey outfit
b1. Skirt
b2. Blouse
b3. Clutch bag

Blue and pink outfit
c1. Trouser suit
c2. Blouse
c3. Hat

Green outfit
d1. Dress
d2. Hooded jacket
d3. Hood lining
d4. Shoulder bag

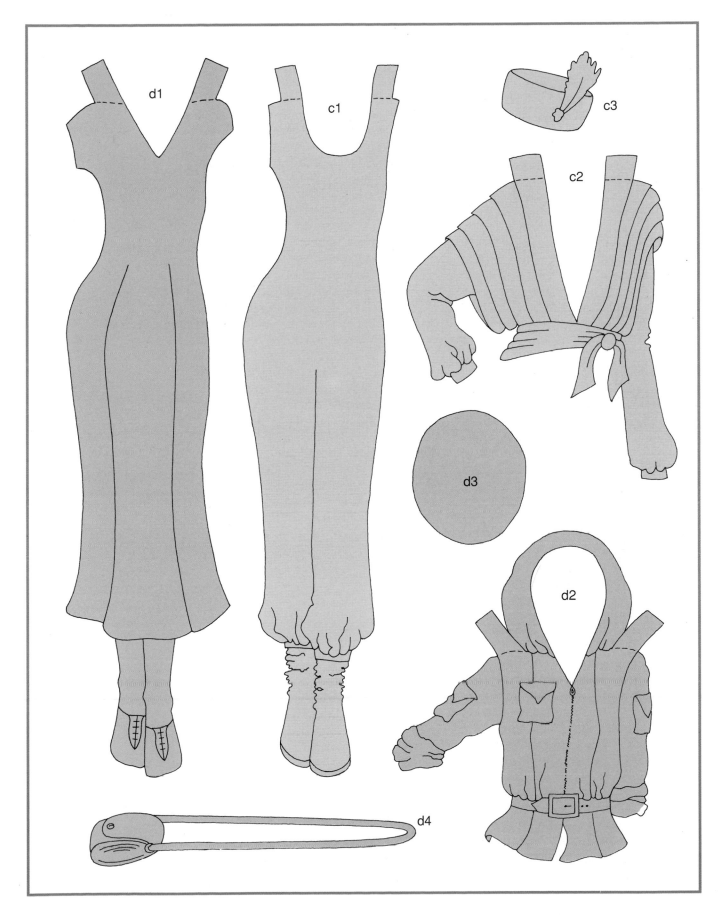

Textures and patterns

The technique used to obtain the dots and stripes on page 55 is 'resist'. In this case I used an art masking fluid (available at most art and craft shops) which becomes rubbery as it dries, but Cow Gum or a sharpened wax crayon can also be used. It is best to practise beforehand and try to get as many variations on the same theme as possible, changing the technique very slightly with each one.

To create the dot pattern put tiny blobs of fluid, varying in size, over the area. Allow the fluid to dry then go over the area with a felt-tipped marker. When this has dried (a matter of seconds) rub away the masking fluid with your finger. You should now have white dots on a coloured background. The dots can be left white or filled in with a contrasting colour.

If the fluid or felt-tipped pen has not quite dried when you rub, a more subtle patterning can be achieved, which in turn gives a more realistic 'fabric look'. Try using different combinations of media and keep all your experiments marked so that they can be referred to later to see how particular effects were made.

The stripes are based on the same principle, but the fluid was trailed across and a deeper shade of green, following the same direction, was lightly scribbled on at intervals as the fluid was drying. The fluid was then rubbed away, leaving some white and some dark-green stripes.

Less spontaneous patterns have to be planned with a little more care. The checks opposite were developed in seven stages. It helps to have a good reference, either the actual fabric or a photograph (from a magazine) which can be carefully scrutinised to decipher colour combinations. This example was taken and adapted from a jacket that appeared in a copy of *Vogue* magazine.

Draw a light grid using a sharp HB pencil, then start filling the squares in with very close lines of colour. Some solid colour is used, as in steps two and six, but most of the area is covered with lines to give a woven effect – this can be seen more clearly on the larger swatch. Once you have mastered the basic idea, colours can be changed and the grid size altered. Plain swatches of colour are positioned against the plaid to see which would best co-ordinate an outfit.

The fake-fur effect is easier. Reference for this was taken from an illustration of a leopard that I found in an animal encyclopaedia. Other furs can be adapted in the same way, breaking down the basic pattern and colour, then building it up again in stages to suit your own requirements.

Having practised and experimented with colours, pattern, texture and media, transfer your chosen design on to thin card and cut out the garment. You may feel confident enough to create the effect of folds in a geometric pattern but if you do not, the shape of the garment and use of greys for shading will indicate the fall of the fabric.

Felt-tipped markers were used for the checks and fur because they have an immediate strength of colour, but they do lack sensitivity, which can be obtained, along with colour strength, by using quality coloured pencils.

Two step-by-step examples of how to produce checks and a fake-fur effect on pieces of card. The references for these were taken from a copy of a Vogue *magazine and an illustrated animal encyclopaedia.*

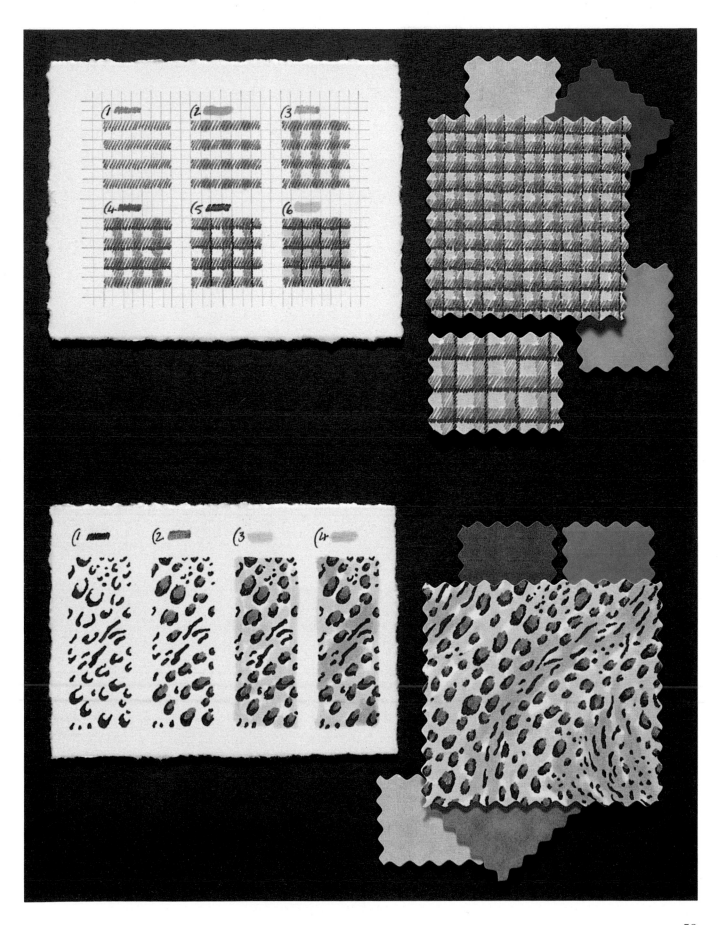

Dancing puppets

The basic pattern for a dancing puppet is shown opposite and this can be adapted slightly for variations in character. The two puppets shown on page 63 are made from mounting board and wallpaper. Out-of-date wallpaper books can be obtained from DIY and similar stores, usually free of charge if you ask nicely! Many of the wallpapers are perfect for dressing puppets and dolls: the ornate, sheeny ones make excellent period costumes; the embossed ones can be used for elaborate circus outfits; flowers can be cut up, as for the ballet dancer; the striped and small-patterned co-ordinating papers are useful for virtually any character. Wallpaper is very pleasurable to use: it is tough but soft and does not crease easily, and it also cuts smoothly and adheres well to the card.

Various magazines are also very useful sources for fabrics, landscapes, interiors and even food; in fact any interesting colour and texture can be cut up and used to create a wonderful collection of character costumes. Old birthday or Christmas cards and quality wrapping paper may also be suitable.

Another idea, using family photographs (you could also use pictures of politicians and other famous or infamous celebrities), is to cut out the heads and stick them on to puppets, then dress them in outrageous clothes.

The basic pattern pieces can be redrawn slightly to accommodate different characters. Ideas for characters can be inspired by illustrations in nursery-rhyme books, books on fables and traditional fairy stories, historical costume books, military books, children's television programmes and fashion magazines.

Materials and equipment

Mounting board; wallpaper; craft knife and blades; cutting board or thick card; glue stick; coloured pencils; darning needle; cotton thread; narrow ribbon; double-sided sticky tape (DSST); very small brass paper studs; a hole punch. Sticks to hold the puppets are optional and narrow beading, with at least one flat side, is the most suitable.

The process of making a wallpaper puppet is best done following this sequence (you can use other paper if you wish but remember that it should be fairly strong):

1. Having traced the pieces on to mounting board, carefully cut them out. Mounting board can be awkward to cut, but with practice and care it becomes as simple as using scissors. Lightly score the pencil line first, then dig a little deeper until the cut is complete, keeping the edge as smooth as possible.

2. When cutting intricate pieces, fingers for example, chip away at the card rather than trying to cut round in a single movement.

3. Stick the darning needle through the centre of each circle.

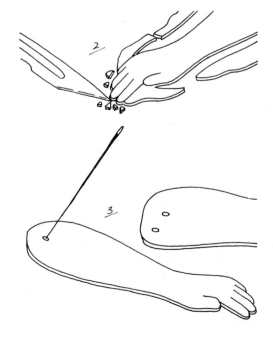

Opposite: Basic pattern pieces for the puppet. The smaller shapes underneath show the adaptations from the original pattern used for the ballerina and jester shown on page 63.

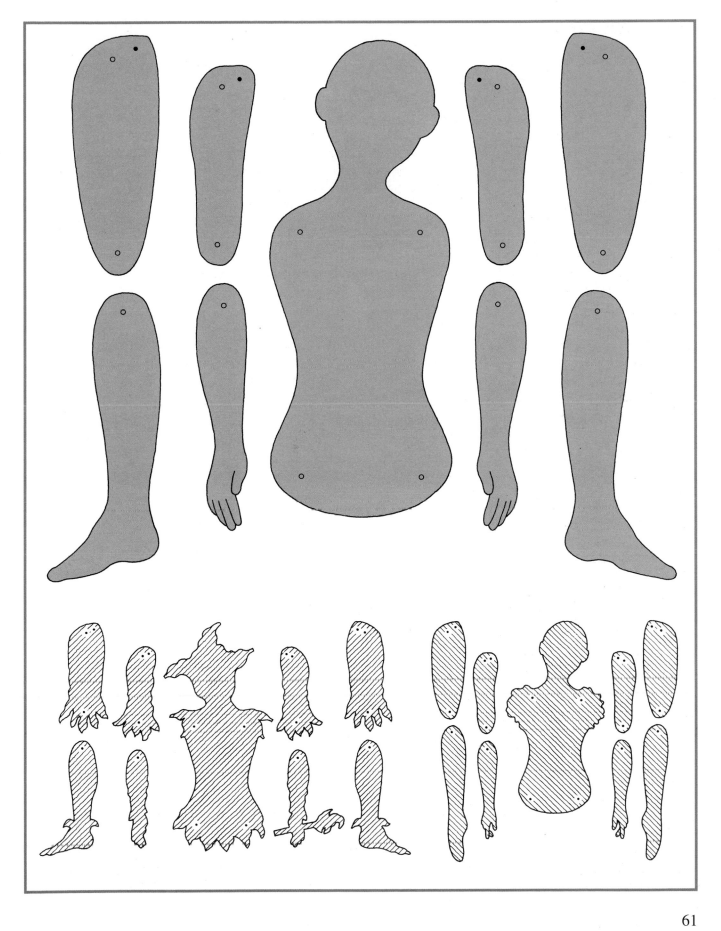

4. Cut the wallpaper pieces larger than the pattern, apply a thin layer of glue, lay the card down and cut round, removing excess paper. (I used a piece of pale-pink writing paper to cover flesh areas.)

5. Using the needle holes as a guide, prick through the wallpaper, then neatly chip out a little square large enough to accommodate the brass stud.

6. Draw features on the face with the coloured pencils.

7. Using the needle and four lengths of appropriately coloured cotton, thread the upper arms together, leaving about 35mm (1½in) slack. Knot both ends. Repeat with the upper legs.

8. Assemble the puppet using the studs but do not flatten the prongs directly against the back of the pieces as this will restrict movement. Instead, push your knife handle (or the blade of a table knife) against the prong, then flatten it.

9. Tie pieces of ribbon to the cotton between the arms and legs. To neaten the top end of the leg ribbon (which would otherwise be seen), stick it down using a thin strip of DSST.

10. It is not necessary to cover the brass stud heads, but it does give a more professional finish. Attach DSST to the back of small pieces of wallpaper and use the hole punch to cut the circles. Remove the backing, then apply to each stud (see the matching studs in the photograph opposite).

11. The puppet is now complete. The arms and legs will swing out when the respective ribbons are pulled. A stick can be attached to the back of the puppet and used as a handle while your other hand pulls the ribbons. Use DSST and, for added strength, a strip of strong adhesive tape to secure the stick.

Wallpaper has been used to make the costumes for the dancing puppets shown opposite, but any patterned, textured or coloured papers can be used.

mobiles

Mobiles

A loose-ringed lampshade frame (available from most craft shops) forms the basic structure for the two mobiles opposite. The patterns on the roundabout were cut from an old wallpaper sample book, then coloured with marker pens. The striped poles (drinking straws) are threaded with fine elastic and a suitably sized coin is secured between each pair of horses – this enables them to bounce slightly, as well as moving round. The mobile will spin backwards and forwards for at least five minutes if spun tightly enough the first time.

Fairground horses are very ornately decorated. They rarely smile and are often rather fearsome, gnashing and champing at the bit. The horses opposite are of a gentler nature and I have kept the decoration to a minimum, using a single motif from the same embossed wallpaper used for the canopy. You could let your imagination run riot and cover them completely with swirls of filigrees.

The bird mobile is a simpler structure built on the bottom loose ring of the lampshade. The little birds are also quite simple to make, though care and patience is required due to the smallness of scale. Having completed the mobile I felt that a large ring would probably have been better, allowing room for two or three more birds. However, large or small the effect is pretty, especially when the mobile turns and catches the light. The gradating foil paper is gift wrapping which I bought from a stationer/gift shop. It was not expensive and actually inspired the design for this particular model. The birds are each weighted with a ceramic bead threaded through the cavity.

The drawings below and on page 68 show other methods of creating mobiles. Weight must be evenly distributed otherwise the mobile will be lop-sided. The horizontal wire structures can be rather dull – endless branches of wire with

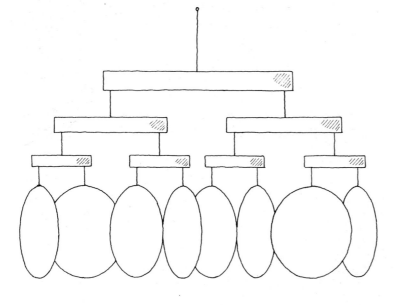

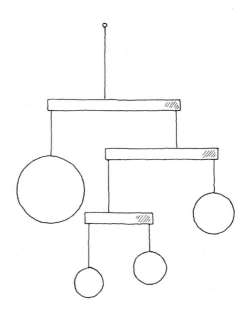

Balance is all-important when creating a mobile, but sound, texture and the effect of light should also be considered. (The circles in the drawing represent various objects.)

66

Two pretty mobiles which turn with the slightest breeze. A little time and patience is required for the making, but the result is well worth while.

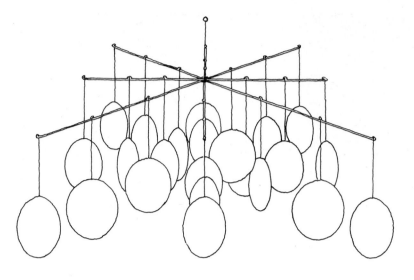

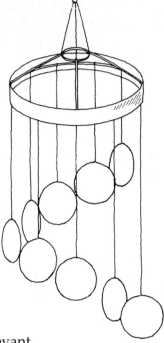

little objects on the end. To add interest I suggest covering the wire with relevant cut-out designs. These should not hinder the free twist of each branch but will, if correctly applied, give the mobile more visual substance.

Other mobiles can be created based on absolute simplicity. The wire becomes part of the design rather than a means to an end. Branches can be used instead of wire. Sophistication and elegance can be achieved by using limited colour or by allowing movement and light to give subtle changes to a single colour. Objects used should always be light enough to be moved by the slightest breeze.

The roundabout

Materials and equipment: Top part of a 250mm (10in) diameter loose-ringed lampshade frame; thin card for the canopy; craft knife; steel-edged rule; cutting mat or thick cardboard; tracing paper and pencil; coloured straws; mounting board – white on one side, grey the other; fine elastic (round rather than flat); double-sided sticky tape (DSST); Cow Gum and a palette knife, or a glue stick; ordinary sticky tape; six coins; fine nylon thread; two brass rings for hanging (one small, one a little larger).

The following items were used to decorate this particular model and can be replaced with your own choice . . . but do use co-ordinated and complementary colours: coloured cartridge paper; coloured tissue paper; thin gold card (only a small amount is required and I used part of an old Easter-egg box); embossed wallpaper; coloured designer marker-pens – these are spirit-based and give a much flatter finish; gold marker pen.

1. Using the pattern opposite, trace both horses (shapes a1 and a2) six times on to the mounting board. Do not trace eyes and mane if you are decorating as in the photograph on page 67. Carefully cut out each horse with the craft knife – this is best done over a long period unless you have exceptionally tough fingers!

Key to diagram on page 69

Roundabout mobile

a1. *Outer horse*
a2. *Inner horse*
a3. *Large mane*
a4. *Small mane*

Bird mobile

b1. *Body*
b2. *Large wings*
b3. *Small wings*
b4. *Tail*

a3

a4

a2

a1

b3

b4

b1

b2

2. Lay one of the a1-shape horses, grey side down, on to the coloured cartridge paper. Roughly draw round the shape then spread a thin film of glue over both the paper and board, wait a minute and then press the two together. Carefully cut away the excess paper. Repeat with the other five a1-shape horses.

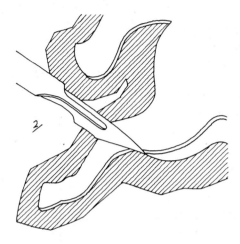

3. Using a spirit-based pen, colour the white sides of all the horses.

4. Cut twelve sets of the horse's mane (shapes a3 and a4) out of the coloured tissue paper. Stick DSST to each piece and attach to the inside of each horse. Using the blunt edge of a kitchen knife, curl the mane (practise beforehand if you have not curled paper before).

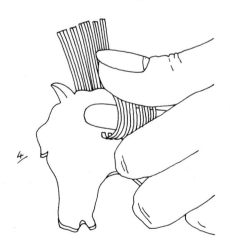

5. Stick DSST on to a piece of gold card and cut small circles for the eyes. (I used a hole punch to make these.) Attach one to each horse.

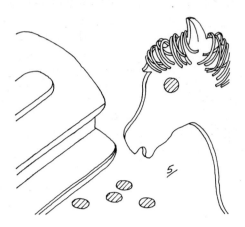

6. Put the horses to one side, laying them on the wrong side to prevent their manes from squashing.

7. Select an appropriate embossed motif wallpaper. The pattern must repeat at least six times. Cut out motifs for the horses and canopy, then colour them accordingly with the spirit-based pens. The shape of the canopy will be set by the shape of your chosen motif.

8. Stick a motif on each a1-shape horse.

9. Measure round the lampshade frame and cut the canopy frill 20mm (³/₄in) longer and 50 to 75mm (2 to 3in) deep. Divide the frill into six equal sections, excluding the 20mm (³/₄in) overlap.

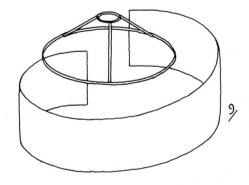

10. Cut and stick strips of coloured cartridge on the frill within the six sections. Draw a gold line between each strip, then attach the six motifs.

11. Turn the frill over and lightly draw a pencil line 15mm (⁵/₈in) from the top. Cut twelve 3 x 15mm (¹/₈ x ⁵/₈in) pieces of mounting board. Using DSST attach

these at regular intervals along the frill on the line. Carefully bend the frill into a circular shape, and join with DSST.

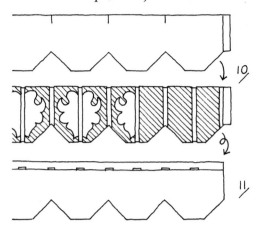

12. The best way of getting the canopy top to fit perfectly is to practise with a few circles of cheap cartridge first. The diameter should be 245mm (9⅝in), but this will vary if your frame is slightly larger or smaller. Divide the circle into twelve segments. Cut and stick coloured cartridge to eleven segments, leaving a gap between each for a gold line.

13. Cut a 38mm (1½in) diameter hole in the centre of the canopy, then cut a line from the centre to the outer edge at

the side of the blank twelfth segment. Attach DSST to this segment and stick it beneath the first to form a shallow cone. Cut a circle of gold card and stick it round the hole at the top of the canopy.

14. Tie three short pieces of nylon thread from the top of the frame to a small brass ring. Fasten a double length of thread from the small ring to the larger one.

15. Cut twelve straws to 150mm (6in). Cut thin strips of coloured cartridge, backed with DSST, and wind one round each straw at a slight angle.

16. Cut twelve 400mm (16in) lengths of elastic. Tie them to the frame, as shown, and thread through a straw. Slit each straw twice at the bottom and pull the elastic into each slit, as shown.

17. Attach DSST to the pen-coloured side of each 'inside' horse. Press the straws and a coin on to this horse, cover them with more DSST and press the 'outer' (decorated) horse down firmly.

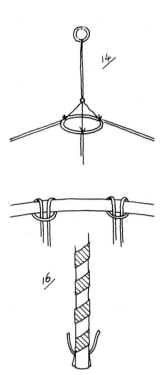

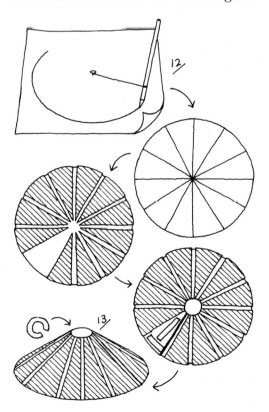

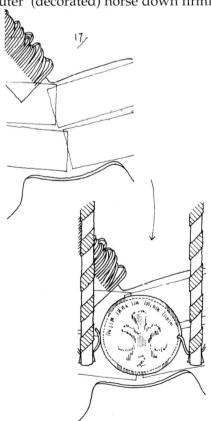

18. Carefully put the frill on the frame, beneath the little card supports. Pull the hanging thread through the hole and let the canopy rest on top of the supports.

The bird mobile

Materials and equipment: Bottom part of a 250mm (10in) diameter loose-ringed lampshade – larger if you want more birds; cheap paper for drawing original cloud design; tracing paper and pencil; thin card for the cloud structure; a sheet of foil gift wrap; pale-coloured cartridge paper for the clouds; thin coloured card for the birds; 8mm ($^5/_{16}$in) ceramic beads, one to fit inside the cavity of each bird; gold marker pen; transparent nylon thread; sewing needle; double-sided sticky tape (DSST); glue stick or Cow Gum and a palette knife; craft knife; cutting mat or thick card; scissors; small brass ring for hanging.

1. Place the lampshade ring on some cheap paper and draw two circles, one round the inside and one round the outside. Now draw in the sun, the silver lining, the sun rays and the clouds.

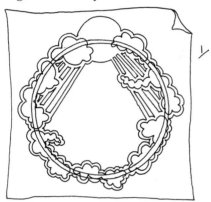

2. Trace everything except the clouds on to a piece of thin card. Stick a second piece of card to the first, sticking DSST in the centre and at the edges, beyond the cloud-formation shape. Carefully cut the two out together using the craft knife. (Practise cutting curves on a spare piece of card). Scissors tend to distort the card, especially in tight corners.

3. Cover one side of one of the cut cards with a thin film of glue and lay it down on the reverse side of the foil paper. Carefully cut out the cloud formation. Now, using the other cut-out, make a second, mirror-image copy – the two

pieces will be fixed back-to-back over the frame.

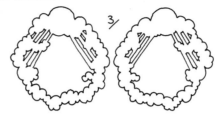

4. Trace and cut out the actual clouds, remembering to reverse the tracing for the second formation. Apply glue and position the clouds on the foil paper.

5. Trace and cut out the bird pieces (shapes b1 to b4 on the diagram on page 69). Lightly score, with the back of the knife, all dotted lines. Remember to mark the dot and slots on the body (b1). Apply gold to the feathers as shown in the photograph on page 67.

6. Stick pieces of DSST to the flaps on the body (b1). Turn the body piece over and position more DSST as shown, but do not stick together yet.

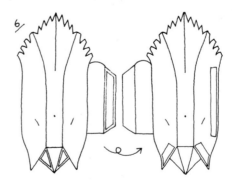

7. Using a length of knotted double nylon, thread a bead as shown. Pass the needle through the dot on the body.

8. Gently bend the scored lines and stick the flaps to form the body shape.

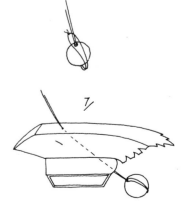

9. Insert the two sets of wings (b2 and b3) into the slits as shown then slide the bead into the body to secure their position. The wings will bend upwards to their final position.

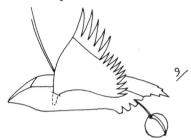

10. Apply some DSST to the tail feathers (b4) as shown and then bend and stick the feathers in place.

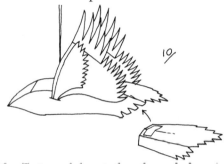

11. Cut and knot the thread, leaving enough to hang from the top of the ring. Repeat the procedure until you have the required number of birds.

12. To hang a second bird on a thread, you will have to make a slot in the underside of the second bird as shown, make a knot, thread the second bead and then continue as before.

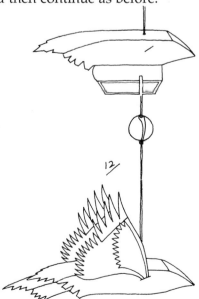

13. Attach the lampshade ring to the back of one of the cloud structures with small pieces of DSST, leaving the top part free. Attach the birds to the ring by looping them round their own thread, as with the bead. It may be necessary to adjust the lengths to avoid the birds' fighting for the same air space. Thread the small ring and attach it to the frame.

14. Secure each thread with DSST and position more pieces around the top edge of the sun and clouds. Gently press the other cloud formation on to the frame. Press the sun and clouds together at the top. The mobile is now complete and ready to be hung.

gift wrap
and tags

Gift wrap and tags

There are so many lovely and varied wrapping papers available these days that it hardly seems worth while attempting to create your own. But there is one very good reason for taking the time and trouble to make the joy of present-giving even nicer. (We are talking here about the gifts that we want to give to those we really care about.) So, having established that the present is given from the heart, the reason for making rather than buying is simply love. A love of creating and a love for the person to whom the gift is given – a favourite grandchild, a doting aunt, a lover or a dear friend. The idea then is not to replicate commercial papers, which would be difficult anyway, but to create something which is 'handmade' and, if at all possible, very personal to the recipient.

Materials and equipment

Almost any kind of paper can be transformed into an imaginative wrapping, but it should not be too thick to fold or too thin to take paint or ink: white or coloured cartridge, lining paper, wallpaper, writing paper, brown paper, rice paper. Thin card is best for the tags. Other materials will depend on your choice of media – paints, pastels, inks, etc., but you will need a craft knife, scissors, a steel-edged rule, a pencil and some cheap paper to practise with.

Personalising

The most obvious way of making paper extra special is to use the recipient's name. This can be written using a variety of media and methods. Some examples are shown on page 78.

1. Take a dark-coloured sheet of cartridge and, using an HB pencil, lightly divide the paper into lines and columns. Write the name in each section using a gold and a silver felt-tipped pen alternately. Turn the paper upside down for each alternate column. Use vertical, diagonal or wavy columns to make a regular pattern.

2. Chalk pastels leave a fine residue of powder on the surface of the paper which can be gently rubbed across the writing to give a soft hazy quality. The name is first written in curved lines all over a dark-coloured paper.

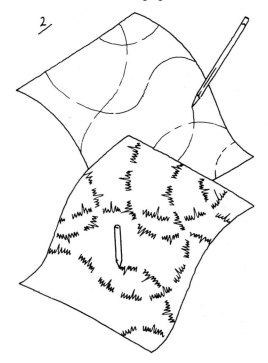

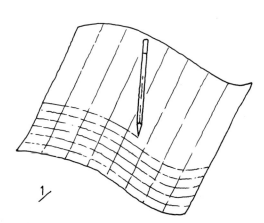

3. Write the name in varying directions all over the paper using three coloured felt-tipped pens held together with sticky tape. This looks very effective when different shades of the same colour are used. For example, pale-pink paper with dark-pink, red and maroon pens.

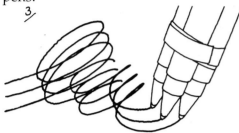

4. Write the name carefully with a tube of liquid glue, then sprinkle it liberally with glitter. Shake any excess glitter on to a clean piece of paper when the glue has dried. Repeat this process, changing the direction of the name each time.

5. If time is plentiful, the name can be formed by cutting out different typefaces (letter styles) from magazines. These are stuck on to a sheet of white paper which is then covered with strips (torn or cut) of pale-coloured tissue paper. A glue stick is ideal for this job.

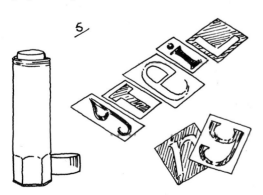

6. The following paste-and-paint method gives very interesting colour and textural effects. Make some cold-water wallpaper paste, using a little less water than instructed on the packet. Mix in a few drops of washing-up liquid. Divide the mixture between two or three shallow bowls and add powder paint, designer's gouache, ink or any other water-based colour to each bowl. Spread the working area with clean, smooth newspaper, lay your paper on top and, using a wide brush, dab the colours all over the surface. Alternatively, spread the mixture on with smooth strokes, working lengthways with one colour and breadthways with another. Write the recipient's name through the paste (this has to be done fairly quickly before the paste dries) using a knitting needle, matchstick, or similar tool.

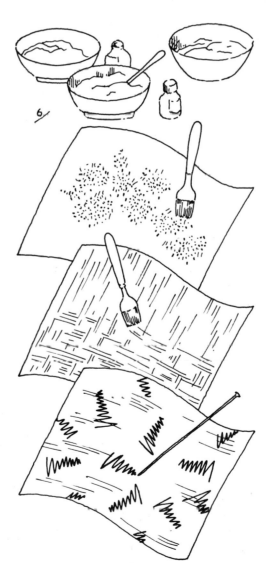

7. Plastic alphabet stencils are available from most art/craft shops. You could make a random pattern or a more formal design with the stencilled name, using coloured pencils, fine charcoal or felt-tipped pens. For a very simple but unusual presentation, wrap the gift carefully in quality brown paper. Stencil the name diagonally across the top corner using a gold felt-tipped pen, then run the pen along the folded edges of the paper. Tie with gold twine or braid. To make a matching tag, fold an oblong of brown paper in half, then edge with the gold pen. Fold a smaller oblong of white or cream paper in half and stick it inside the brown. Write your message, thread the twine through and attach the tag to the gift.

8. If you feel adept with a craft knife try printing the name, or initials, using finely grained polystyrene pieces (often used in packing). The polystyrene gives a lively, uneven texture. Cheap pencil erasers are also good for printing and give a smoother, more accurate finish.

Ideas for ornate initials are to found in books on typography which can be borrowed from most libraries. Dry-transfer-lettering catalogues are also a good source of reference for all kinds of typefaces. These can be bought at most art/design shops.

Water-based printing inks are available from craft shops, but gouache or powder paints are reasonably good alternatives. It is useful, but not necessary, to have a printing roller. This is rolled over the paint and then over the reversed image cut from the polystyrene or rubber. An even coat of paint is obtained with a roller but careful use of a paintbrush would suffice.

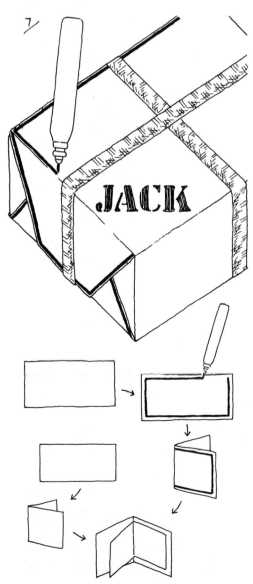

There are many ways of making gift-wrap more personal to the recipient; writing his or her name is one of them. (Opposite.)

79

Another way of personalising your wrapping paper is to reflect in some way the recipient's hobbies, passions or interests. The design should also relate to the gift, of course – a beautifully designed and co-ordinated paper and matching tag, suggesting a strong nautical theme might look rather odd with a book on Ancient Chinese Homoeopathy! But then, maybe not? I am all for breaking rules and if you feel inclined to put two disparate subjects together, then do so.

I like really zany ideas. For example, a keen gardening friend would receive *The History of an English Garden* wrapped in a floral print wallpaper with a Wellington boot print on both sides, and tied with garden twine. A slightly tamer version of this is shown in the photograph opposite. The small boot print was cut from polystyrene and printed on to wallpaper. The top of the tag was trimmed with the same paper and the sole was cut from a piece of sweet-wrapper foil.

The wrapped gift in the photograph covered with 'real' kisses was quite an adventure. While trying to achieve a good lip print, I sensed someone watching through the window. How do you explain to an astonished son the reason for kissing a piece of paper and having lipstick smudged over the lower face and nose? (If you try this, do watch out for unwanted nose and chin prints.)

The heart-shaped tag is simply three co-ordinating papers, cut successively smaller, stuck together with the top one folding back to reveal a message. The lip print was cut from a practice sheet.

Angling is obviously the subject of the last wrapping paper and tag in the photograph. The wave effect was achieved by using a card mask and spraying ink through a diffuser (these can be bought from art/craft shops.)

To produce a similar design you will need: a large unvarnished board, a large sheet of cartridge paper, a similarly sized sheet of card for the mask, some newspaper to protect the surrounding area, gummed brown-paper tape, adhesive tape, diffuser, inks and rubber gloves.

1. Stick the paper to the board using brown-paper tape on all four sides. Wet the paper gently with a sponge, taking up excess water. Leave to dry.

2. Draw a line of waves across the middle of the card, then cut in half.

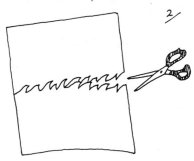

3. It is easier to work with the board tilted at an angle, so put plenty of newspaper over the working area and position the board.

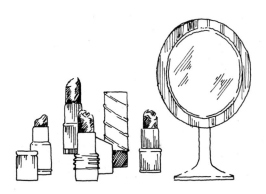

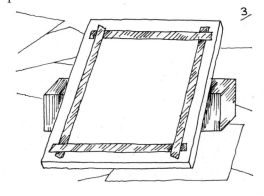

The top and bottom gift-wrap papers are designed to reflect hobbies and interests. The centre paper is obviously for someone very special.

4. Stick both pieces of the mask to the top of the board, leaving a gap of approximately 25mm (1in).

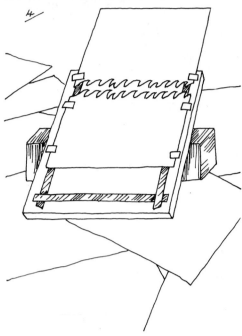

6. Move the mask down so that top piece covers the area just sprayed. Continue applying sprayed ink (using different tones) until paper is covered.

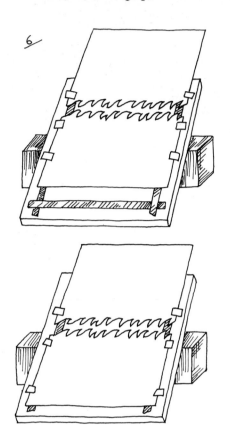

5. Spray with ink by placing the diffuser in a bottle of ink and blowing through the horizontal tube. (Practise this first on spare paper.)

Note The card will become 'baggy' due to continual wetting with ink. If you hold it gently against the paper with a rubber-gloved hand the result will be sharper.

This spray-and-mask technique can be used to achieve many other types of all-over designs.

Gift tags

Gift tags should always look as if they belong to the wrapping paper, either by design, or by colour, or by both. Their construction can be very simple, like those shown in the photographs, or you could attempt smaller versions of the greetings cards that are described on pages 86 to 101. However, these do involve more intricate folding and cutting methods. A simple tag with a folding letter inside is made as follows:

1. Cut a 50 x 100mm (2 x 4in) rectangle out of white or pale-coloured paper. Cut another oblong from thin card, in a contrasting colour and slightly larger. Fold both in half.

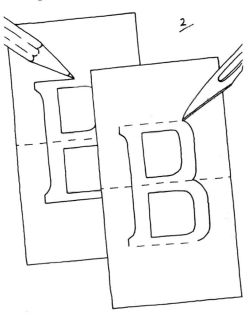

2. Draw a letter in the middle of the paper. Carefully cut round it but leave the top and bottom attached.

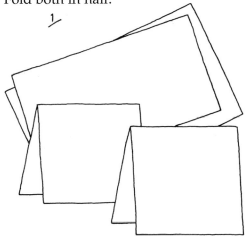

3. Carefully push the letter so that the inverted crease comes out as shown.

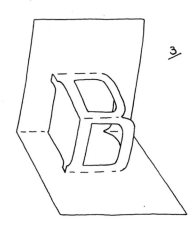

4. Close the paper to crease the letter at top and bottom.

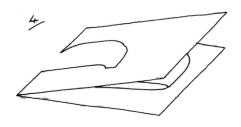

5. Open the paper and place it inside the card, securing with dabs of glue.

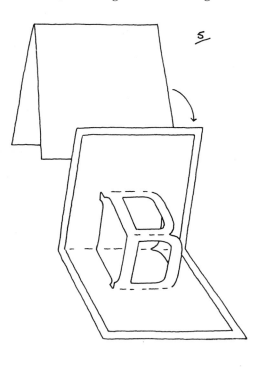

greeting
cards

Greeting cards

It is not known where or when the idea of sending cards of greeting began – many romantic possibilities spring to mind, but we shall never know. However, English Christmas cards were being produced on a large scale by the 1860s and took advantage of the new 'Penny Post'. At first simple, idealistic illustrations were printed on single pieces of card; then the structure became very elaborate, and involved clever methods of folding and cutting.

Nowadays many people believe commercialism has gone mad. We have (say the rapacious card manufacturers) many reasons for sending a greeting: whether you have just failed your driving test for the ninth time, recently broken your leg or hope soon to become a great-great-grandparent, there is a card specifically for you. However, making your own cards for such occasions can be rewarding – and can also save you considerable expense.

Handmade cards which have, as part of their design, an oblique or blatant reference to the recipient give an extra-special dimension. Space will not allow a presentation of ideas to suit every individual but, with a little imagination, the following cards can be adapted to accommodate the quirks of an eccentric aunt or the simple needs of a three-year-old.

Most of the examples shown have a three-dimensional aspect and some involve folding and cutting. Once the basic principles have been understood, you can go on to create your own designs. It is advisable to make a dummy from cheap paper before going on to produce the final version.

A few suggestions for written messages have been given – some may be considered slightly insulting, but not if the recipient has a sense of humour!

Remember to design your card so that it will fit comfortably into an envelope. If you carefully unstick a commercial envelope and look at the way it has been cut and constructed, you can make your own. Using your card measurements as a guide, plus a little extra, adapt the shape of the commercial envelope to fit. If possible, use a coloured paper which complements the colours in the design.

Once again I have made use of the wallpaper sample books for this chapter. I strongly recommend anyone with an interest in papercraft work to obtain some. Pictures from magazines have also been used – so beg or borrow and start a collection. Home-shopping catalogues are equally useful.

Materials and equipment

This is a general list; other items will be needed for individual cards. Some card (a range of colours and weights is available from most art/craft shops); steel-edged rule; craft knife; scissors; glue; double-sided sticky tape (DSST); pencil.

Comb in cardigan pocket

Perhaps suitable for an avuncular sort of chap or a great-grandfather? You could also send it to someone (with whom you share the same sense of humour) who is bald . . . attach a lock of hair inside and write above it 'some hair for your comb!' Underneath as a sweetener you could add, '(75% of all women find bald men irresistibly attractive)'.

To make the card you will need: items listed at the beginning of this chapter; thick card for the buttons; textured wallpaper which has a knitted appearance, and a comb.

1. Cut the card to the required size. Score it in half with the blunt edge of your craft knife, then fold.

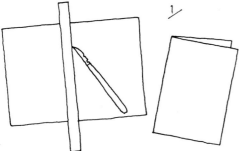

2. Cut a piece of the wallpaper slightly smaller than the card and glue it as indicated. Cut a narrow slit for the comb.

3. Cut a piece of wallpaper to fit down the side of the card; include flaps as shown. Fold and stick the flaps underneath, to form a double thickness, then stick the strip on to the card.

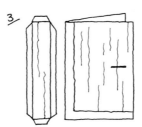

4. Cut the bottom and pocket welts in a similar way and attach them to the card. The pocket welt should cover the slit.

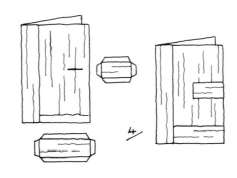

From left to right:
Comb in cardigan.
Three-dimensional town.
Dead flowers – with a
surprise seed packet.

5. Draw four circles on to the thick card then cut them out using a knife or scissors. Smooth the edges with an emery board. Draw an inner circle, four holes and some fine thread with a dark pen. Choose colours similar to the cardigan and shade in, leaving white highlights. I used spirit-based markers but the same effect can be achieved with pencils.

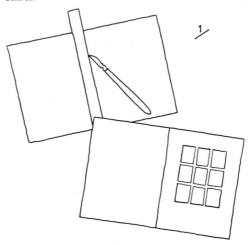

6. Stick the buttons on to the welt, slide the comb into the slit, then write your message inside.

Dead flowers

The left-hand message inside this card could read: 'I bought you some flowers for your birthday (or anniversary, etc.) but they died ...' Then on the right-hand side, attach a little packet of flower seeds and write: '... so here's the next best thing'.

To make the card you will need: items listed at the beginning of this chapter; a small-patterned wallpaper; a paper doily; tracing paper; a piece of clear acetate; a suitable outdoor picture (from an old Christmas card); a picture of a vase and a packet of flower seeds.

My vase was cut from a catalogue. It was originally a nice vase of tulips. I cut the tulips off then cut the leaves and repositioned them to hang down. I gently rubbed the leaves with a spirit-based marker which dissolved the printing ink and made the leaves look slightly withered – this can be drawn if a picture is unavailable.

1. Cut the card to the required size. Score it in half with the blunt edge of your knife. Carefully measure and cut out a window frame on the front of the card.

2. Cut the wallpaper to fit the card, cut out a rectangle that is slightly larger than the window frame, and then stick the wallpaper on to the card. Attach a piece of doily beneath the window. Glue down your vase of flowers.

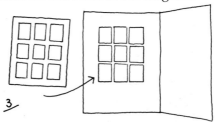

3. Using a colour to complement the wallpaper, cut another window frame with panes smaller than the original. Now, working inside the card, stick this frame on the back of the original.

4. Lay a piece of acetate over the frame, to give an appearance of glass, using neat strips of DSST to attach it to the card. Repeat with a piece of tracing

paper to dull the picture. Cut the picture a little larger than the tracing paper and acetate, then attach as before.

5. Another piece of paper is needed to cover the edges of the picture and the ridges made by the tracing and acetate. Again using a colour to complement the wallpaper, cut and stick a frame as shown. Attach the seed packet to the right-hand side and write your message.

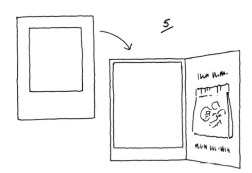

Three-dimensional town

This example demonstrates one of the simplest methods of three-dimensional work in card making. The front of this particular card has a paintbrush attached (using DSST) and a small pot of red paint drawn in the corner. The caption reads, 'On your birthday...' and continues inside '... paint the town RED!' I used plain white writing paper for the town sections.

1. Cut the card to the required size. Score it in half with the blunt edge of your craft knife, then fold.

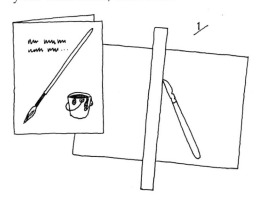

2. Make a light pencil mark in the middle of each inside flap. Measure the distance between these two marks and subtract 10mm ($^3/_8$in) – this measurement will be the maximum length of your model. The other two sections will get progressively narrower and taller.

3. Cut the sections out, including a flap at each side. Draw your chosen scene then, using your craft knife, carefully cut the outline of the buildings and some tiny windows.

4. Lightly score the flaps, attach DSST, fold them back and then make a light pencil mark at the centre of each section.

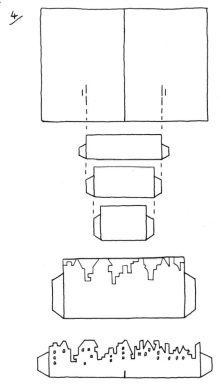

5. With the card open flat, match the centre marks of the tallest section with the centre fold of the card, then stick down firmly. Carefully close the card to crease the section in half. Open it and position the next section about 25mm (1in) lower. Close again to crease it, then repeat with the final section.

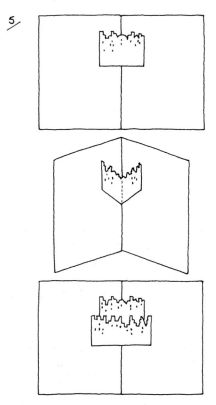

The background for this card was made by sticking squares of varying shades of blue (for the sky) and green (for the grass) on to the card. The squares – 712 in all – were cut from magazines and catalogues. The process was time-consuming but enjoyable. Alternatively, you could use a whole section of sky, green fields, seascapes, townscapes or any manner of images. Holiday brochures usually have a good supply of skies.

Frog

This is another three-dimensional method which can easily be adapted. The mouth of the frog here is quite small, but it can be made as large as your card will allow. Different animals can be used and you could try folding the card into three, then having a dialogue between two people.

To make the frog card you will need: items listed at the beginning of this chapter; a piece of sturdy white writing paper; Cow Gum; small palette knife; torn strips of coloured tissue paper; two green felt-tipped markers; a black marker pen; coloured card for the backing. I have drawn a small picture of a waving figure in the frog's mouth, but you could replace it with a photograph of yourself, or the recipient, or anything appropriate to the recipient.

1. Cut your paper to the required size. Fold it in half, make a sharp crease, then crease it again backwards. Open it flat and trace or copy the frog. Draw over the lines with a black marker.

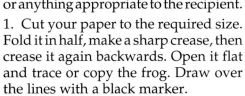

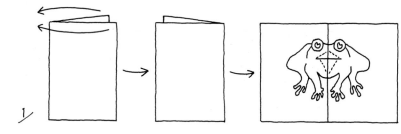

Use this full-size pattern for the frog card.

2. Using the palette knife, apply a thin film of Cow Gum across the paper just above the frog. Quickly but carefully position a strip of tissue paper, apply another film of Cow Gum over the top, then slide the flat side of the palette knife along the tissue to squeeze out excess gum or air bubbles.

Repeat until all the strips are positioned, slightly overlapping one another. Leave until dry then rub the gum off with your finger, taking care not to tear the tissue. (It is a good idea to

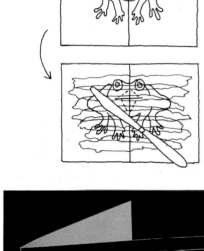

practise this before embarking on the final card.)

3. Colour the frog with the two green pens. Do this roughly so that areas of tissue show through. Cut a horizontal slit for the frog's mouth.

4. Fold the paper back as shown. Fold the mouth back to make two triangles, then turn the paper round and fold again. Open the paper out, then slowly fold it the correct way, pushing the mouth pieces towards you.

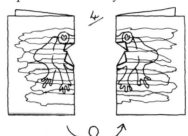

From left to right:
Earring – the other one is sent in a pretty gift box.
Frog – who has swallowed the sender.
Cup of tea – with an extra tea bag for the strong at heart!

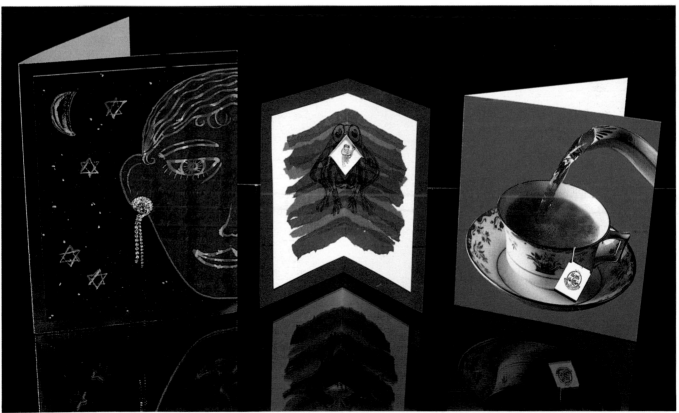

5. Cut the coloured card, a little larger than the paper, and score it in half using the blunt edge of a knife. Lay the paper on top, matching the centre creases, then, using a pencil, mark through the mouth to get the position for your picture.

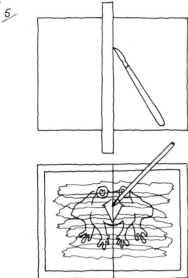

6. Glue the picture on to the card. Turn the frog over and stick pieces of DSST next to the centre crease, as shown. Carefully attach to the card.

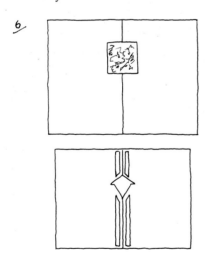

Earring

This is a very glamorous card, but the earring does not need to be expensive. The other earring could be given or sent separately in a pretty gift box. Earrings with hooks are easier to attach to the card because they lie flat. If you want to use the shaft type with a stud, you will need a strip of polystyrene packing to prevent it from piercing through the back of the card, the envelope and possibly the postman! Glue the narrow packing along the inside edge of the card. The multi-coloured effect is achieved by drawing coloured stripes with felt-tipped pens on to the white card, then painting the images with household bleach on to dark tissue paper after it has been stuck to the card.

To make the card you will need: items listed at the beginning of this chapter; some gold card; some black and purple tissue paper; four coloured felt-tipped markers, preferably spirit-based with a wide tip (I used orange, green, red and blue); a gold marker; some household bleach; a small paintbrush; Cow Gum; palette knife.

1. Cut the gold card to the required size. Score it in half with the blunt edge of a knife, then fold. Cut a piece of white card that is 10mm (^{3}/$_8$in) smaller on three sides.

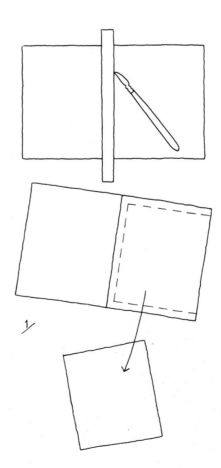

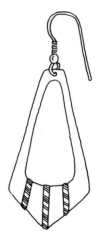

Please refer to the instructions on your container of household bleach before using. Always keep bleach out of the reach of children.

2. Lay the purple tissue over the black and lightly draw the outline of half a face. Hold the two papers firmly on your cutting board and carefully cut the outline. You should now have two backgrounds and two half-faces which fit perfectly together. (You could use the purple background and the black face for another card.)

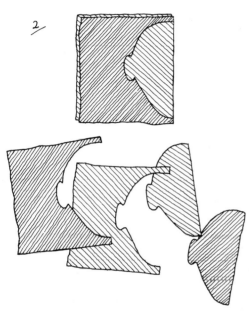

3. Lightly draw the face outline on the white card, then colour the area with stripes using the markers. Draw a moon and four stars loosely (i.e., not too accurately) in blue or green.

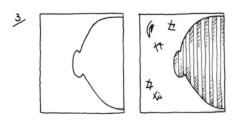

4. Quickly apply a thin film of Cow Gum over the entire surface of the white card (which should be on a piece of spare paper to protect the working surface). Carefully position the black tissue, then the purple, then quickly apply another film of gum over the top and slide the flat side of your palette knife over the surface. This will squeeze out air bubbles and excess gum. Leave to dry for ten minutes, then, using your

fingertips, carefully roll the gum off the surface. The tissues should now be perfectly flat. Trim any excess from the edges. (If you have never used Cow Gum with tissue paper before, practise the above method beforehand.)

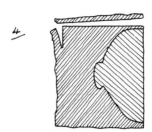

5. Now comes the fun! Carefully pour some bleach into a small container. Using a soft pencil draw an eye, eyebrow, half a nose and mouth and some hair. Lift the card up to the light and you should be able to see where you drew the moon and stars. Loosely draw over them with the pencil.

Dip your brush into the bleach and paint over the pencil lines. In a few seconds the colour of the tissue will disappear, to be replaced with more subtle colour shades. Drop some little dots of bleach on to the black to indicate smaller stars. When the bleach has dried (about five minutes) carefully rub out the pencil. Using a gold pen, outline the face and highlight the moon and stars.

6. Stick strips of DSST on to the back of the white card and attach it to the gold card. Make a small hole with the point of your craft knife, then push the earring through.

Cup of tea

This card contains a tea bag to make a nice cup of tea for the recipient. It was a stroke of luck when I found the picture while searching through a pile of magazines and catalogues. The idea had been to find a smaller cup and saucer, then enlarge it on a photo-copying machine and cover it with coloured cellophane – which is what you could do if you cannot find one large enough to accommodate the tea-bag tag.

To make the card you will need: the items listed at the beginning of this chapter; a good reference of a cup and saucer; easy access to a photocopier; small pieces of yellow cellophane and tracing paper; brown and yellow felt-tipped pens; a tea bag; a sewing needle. Crockery catalogues are a good source of reference. If your reference cup and saucer is small, use a photocopier to enlarge to the right size.

1. Carefully cut the cup and saucer out and stick it on to the card. Draw in the outlines of the spout, the pouring tea and the tea in the cup. Look very closely at the pouring tea (page 91) then, using brown and yellow markers, make similar areas of colour, leaving some white highlights. Repeat with the tea in the cup.

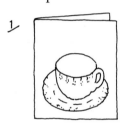
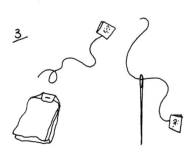

2. Cut a piece of yellow cellophane to fit over the pouring tea and a piece of tracing paper to fit the tea in the cup. Stick these on with a thin film of glue. (The tracing paper will dull the colour to give an effect of added milk; the cellophane will sharpen the colour of the pouring tea and give a transparent appearance.)

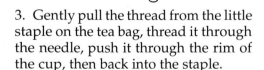

3. Gently pull the thread from the little staple on the tea bag, thread it through the needle, push it through the rim of the cup, then back into the staple.

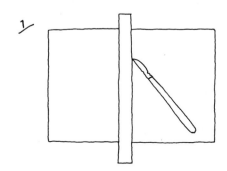

4. Hitch the thread up on the inside of the card with a small piece of sticky tape if the tea bag hangs below the bottom of the card.

5. If you want to colour the cup and saucer use pencils or water-based felt-tipped pens. Spirit-based pens will dissolve and smudge your photocopy.

Silk handkerchief

Attention to detail will give this card credence. You will need: items listed at the beginning of this chapter; a small piece of thin, white copy paper; black cartridge paper; shiny black card and a small piece of shiny white card (for the buttons); black tissue paper or cartridge for the tie; a hole punch for the buttons; a silk handkerchief. Refer to the diagram opposite for the shapes of the pieces of card and paper.

1. Score the white card in half using the blunt edge of a knife.

Key to diagram on page 95

Silk handkerchief
a1. Card shape
a2. Collar
a3. Jacket
a4. Lapel
b1. Shirt front
c1. Bow tie (back)
c1. Bow tie (front)
c3. Bow tie (knot)

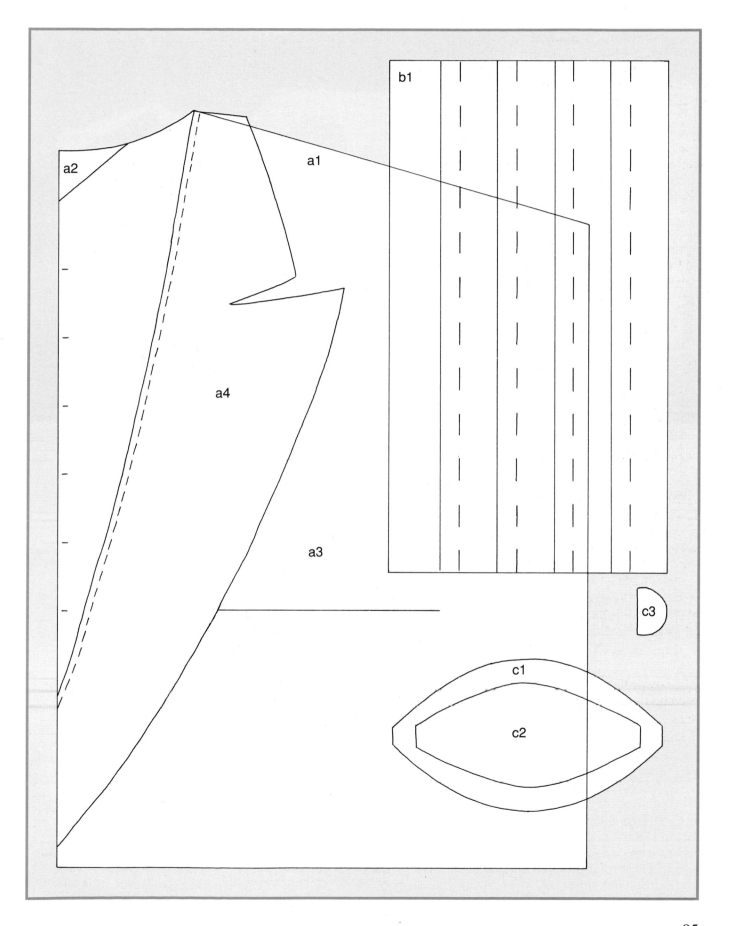

a2

a1

a4

a3

b1

c3

c1

c2

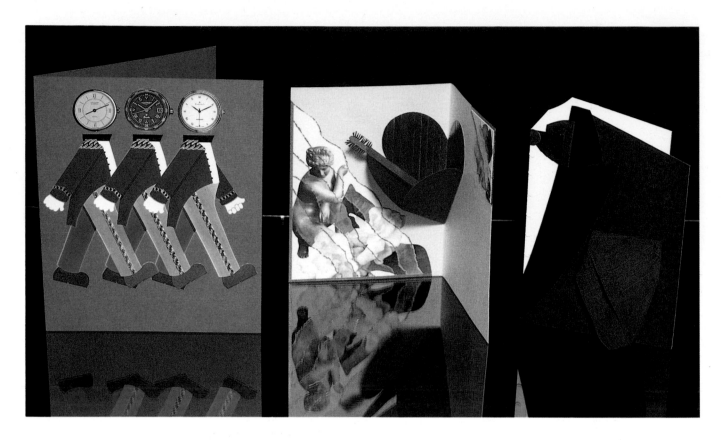

2. Cut the card to the shape (a1). Slit the top edge open so that the tips of the collar (a2) can be folded outwards. Cut off the other corner.

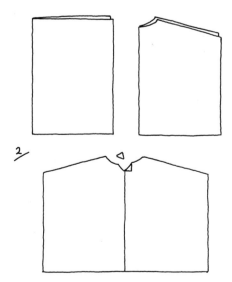

3. Cut the thin white paper for the shirt (b1) to the size shown on the diagram. Lightly draw the solid lines on the facing side and the broken lines on the reverse side (draw the latter as solid lines). Concertina-fold the paper. The easiest way to do this is to lay your rule along the first solid line, fold the paper upwards against the rule, remove the rule, then crease sharply. Turn the paper over, lay the rule on the next line and proceed as before, reversing the paper each time. When all the creases have been made press them down together.

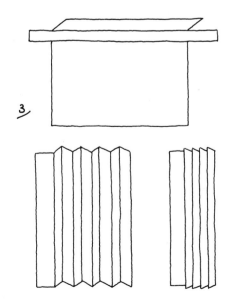

From left to right:
Marching time.
Valentine card.
Silk handkerchief.

4. Use pieces of sticky tape to secure the pleats in position. Lay the paper on the diagram (a1) and draw a line just beyond the dotted line. Cut excess paper off. Using DSST, stick the shirt front on to the card just below the folded collar.

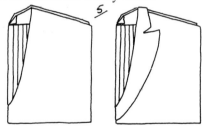

5. Cut the body of the jacket (a3), up to the dotted line, out of the black cartridge. Attach it to the card using DSST. Cut out and attach the lapel (a2), taking care not to mark the shiny card.

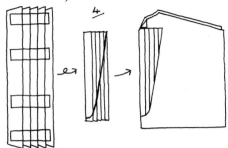

6. Open the card flat and cut the pocket slit.

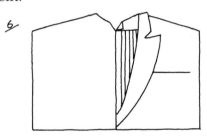

7. Cut the bow-tie pieces (c1 and c2) from tissue or cartridge. Fold them in half, using DSST to secure. Stick the two pieces together, then attach to the card. Cut a thin piece of card for the knot (c3), then stick tissue or cartridge on top. Stick neatly on to the bow.

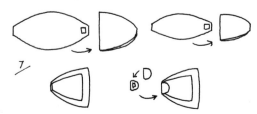

8. Fold the handkerchief and pull it through the slit. Carefully fold any excess fabric at the back and secure with neat pieces of sticky tape.

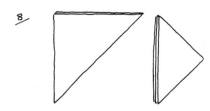

Valentine card

An arrow through the heart seems to me a rather cruel declaration of love, but tradition dictates the symbol so here it is. The card itself, the heart and the arrow are all made from stiff card. To give some texture to the inside of the heart I cut two red dresses from a magazine, one satin and one finely embroidered. These were cut into strips and glued alternately on to the heart. The white roses and statue were also taken from magazines. I glued them on to a piece of pale-cream card, tore strips of tracing paper and glued them over the pictures, then ran a gold pen along the torn edges of the tracing paper. The arrow lies flat when the card is closed and moves up as the card is opened.

To make the card you will need: the items listed at the beginning of this chapter; dark-cream, light-cream and red card; white photocopy paper or thin cartridge; appropriate cut-outs from magazines; tracing paper; a gold felt-tipped pen; a red pencil or pen.

1. Cut the dark-cream card to roughly 180 x 280mm (7 x 11in). Lightly score with the blunt edge of a knife then fold in half. Trace the heart (without flaps) on to the photocopy paper. Turn it over, hold it up to the light and redraw – this only needs to be a rough guideline.

2. Fold the paper so that the crease goes through the centre of the heart. Draw a thick red line over the crease.

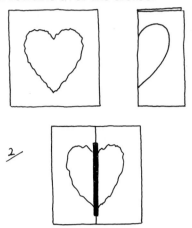

3. Cut strips of red from magazines roughly 6mm (¼in) wide. Starting from the middle, a little way from the crease

but overlapping the thick red line, stick the strips over the roughly drawn heart. When the heart has been covered, turn the paper over and cut the heart out. Stick it on to the card, making sure the centre creases match.

Full-size pattern for the Valentine card.

4. Trace the heart (including flaps) on to the red card. Cut it out, then lightly score and fold the flaps and the centre. Attach strips of DSST to the flaps, bend them back and stick carefully over the heart on the card. Close and open the card to ensure that all creases are central.

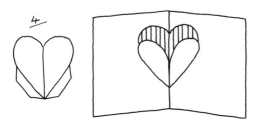

5. Cut various relevant pictures from magazines; these could be generally romantic or specific to the recipient. Stick them on to the pale-cream card. Tear strips of tracing paper, glue them over the pictures, then draw along the edges with gold pen.

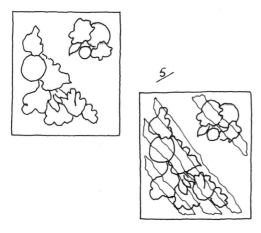

6. Draw sets of right-angled lines through the pictures, as shown, then cut out the two corners.

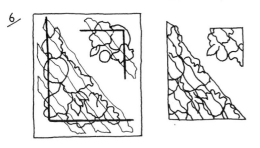

7. Lay the corners on to the card, mark their position, remove again and then colour the edges of the card with a gold

pen. When the gold has dried, glue the corners in position.

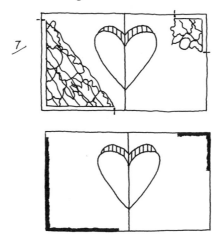

8. Trace the arrow on to red card. Cut it out and colour the shaft gold, on both sides, then allow to dry. Fold the shaft as shown. Attach a small piece of DSST and position the shaft inside the folding heart. You may have to try this once or twice to get the position exactly right. The arrow should not be seen when the card is closed and it should lift up smoothly as the card opens.

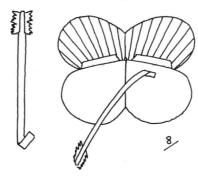

Marching time

An abundance of watch and jewellery advertisements in my collection of old magazines gave me the idea for this card. You could write on the front 'Time marches on . . .', then on the inside something like, '. . . but you remain the same, youthful, charming', etc. Or, if you want to be cheeky '. . . and it certainly shows!' perhaps tempered with (unless you mean it!) 'but I still love you' or 'you're still wonderful'.

The card is very simple to make. You will need basic items listed at the beginning of this chapter; tracing paper; coloured felt-tipped markers or pencils (see the note after step 3 regarding markers.)

1. Cut a 225 x 360mm (9 x 14in) piece of card. Score it in half with the blunt edge of a knife, then fold. Find three watches of similar size and carefully cut them out.

2. Trace the soldiers on to white paper then colour them in. Find some gold chains (home-shopping catalogues are very good for these and other pieces of jewellery). Cut them out and stick them as braid down the outside leg, round the sleeves and on top of the shoulders.

3. Cut the soldiers out carefully. Stick them on to the card, leaving enough room at the top for the watches and at the bottom for your message. Stick the watches a little way above the uniform collars.

Note Water-based markers are fine, but they tend to be streaky. Spirit-based ones usually give a good flat colour but they do tend to bleed on the paper.

This is a dilemma. In order to achieve a flat colour *and* clean edges I used spirit-based markers but cut out each section of the uniform as individual pieces and then stuck each piece down separately, one on top of the other.

It is rather time-consuming and not necessary unless you are a raving

Full-size pattern for marching time card. Can be used as a single piece or cut as individual soldiers.

perfectionist, like myself! The slight three-dimensional effect is achieved by running a grey marker down against the sleeve, where it lies on the jacket bodice; and between each pair of legs. You should also draw a thinner line of the same colour at the bottom edge of each sleeve.

Postscript

With regard to my own card-making attempts, I have to admit that what with an ever-increasing family and full-time teaching, there is seldom enough time to make cards for every occasion. But I do try to make a concerted effort at Christmas (and I often say, never again!) producing about sixty cards for family, friends and colleagues – some of which are shown above. A small production line is set up and I work every evening for two weeks. Each card is carefully cut out, drawn or painted then glued and assembled, put into an envelope (also often handmade) and finally posted. The one dilemma is that people come to expect this annual ornament and when, for some very good reason, creative cards have been omitted from the pre-Christmas agenda, pertinent remarks are not appreciated, as one staggers out of the festive period muttering, 'Thank goodness it's only once a year.' But . . . there is no doubt that people are touched by the giving of something which has been created by the giver. It produces an added sense of caring and love – qualities we are much in need of today. So handmade cards or gifts are well worth the effort.

A selection of handmade Christmas cards, from left to right:

Last year's card (since I am now more environmentally aware) has a simple message: under Santa on his sledge it reads, 'save our planet'; inside, the sledge is being pulled by a bus and underneath, 'use public transport'.

The small card has an origami Santa inside.

I used overlapping, textured white paper, a simple embossing method and some silver gift wrap to create the snow scene.

101

candle
shades

Candle shades

This chapter demonstrates another dimension of papercraft with the introduction of light. I have chosen candle shades rather than lampshades because they do not involve the use of a frame and somehow, the gentle flickering light of a candle gives a greater sense of intimacy and comfort. The shades are not difficult to make but some require more delicate craftsmanship and patience than others.

I cannot over-emphasise the care that should be taken when using candles. If the following precautions are taken the shades will be perfectly safe:

1. Use only the small candles which sit in a little metal case – these can be bought quite cheaply at some craft shops or shops which specialise in oriental products.

2. Never use a candle alone; always put it in a clear, thick glass jar which is taller than the flame – this will prevent danger from draughts. Neat little jars can usually be purchased from the same source as the candles.

3. Never leave a lighted candle and shade unattended, and certainly never within the reach of a curious child.

Paper for the shades should be neither so thick as to prevent the light from coming through nor so thin that the shade cannot stand unaided. If a paper does seem too weak (a typing or photocopy paper for example), a band of slightly thicker paper, stuck round the top and bottom edges, will help to secure its structure. Almost any paper which fulfils these two criteria can be used: white or pastel-coloured cartridge, textured writing paper or handmade papers. I have included drafting film, acetate and coloured cellophane because their translucent or transparent qualities mean that they lend themselves perfectly to uses with light.

Materials and equipment

Gluing is often a matter of personal preference. I used double-sided sticky tape to join the seams of the shades and a recently introduced dry adhesive, which comes in sheet form, to stick shapes to the walls of the shades. The following list of basic equipment will be needed to make any of the shades described. A more specific list of equipment and materials is given just before the step-by-step instructions for each shade. You will need: a cutting mat; steel-edged rule; craft knife and blades; sharp, pointed scissors; HB pencil; sharpener (always use a sharp point); eraser; double-sided sticky tape (DSST).

Handmade paper shades

Indian or Japanese handmade paper gives such a lovely and interesting effect that it needs no other ornament or decoration. The papers are made from diverse natural materials: jute, straw, flowers, hemp, banana leaves, husks or even algae; they come in different weights (thickness) and finishes (rough and smooth). The only problem is getting it. If your local art/craft shop cannot help, try contacting the art/design department of your nearest college. Alternatively, you could try making your own – there are lots of books on this subject and details of some are included at the back of this book.

To make a shade simply cut an accurate rectangle which will fit comfortably round the small candle jar mentioned in the introduction, or a jam jar. Stick a strip of DSST down one edge and join the two sides together. Do this carefully to prevent creasing the paper (practise with some cheap paper first). If you have a firm cylinder to hand, a thick rolling pin for example, use it as a support so that firm pressure can be applied to the join without the risk of permanently distorting the shade.

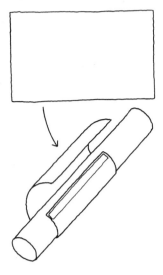

Three simple candle shades created from pieces of handmade paper.

Concertina shade

This shade was made with a parchment-type paper which can be bought from most art and craft shops. To make it you will need an A3 (12 x 16½in) sheet of paper and the materials listed at the beginning of this chapter.

1. Cut the sheet to an approximate height of 250mm (10in). Using a sharp pencil lightly mark 20mm (¾in) sections along the top and bottom edges. Turn the paper over and repeat.

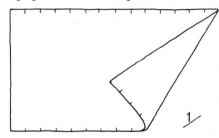

2. Lay your rule to match the first set of marks. Press the rule down firmly then lift the paper to form a crease. Remove the rule and press the crease carefully but firmly with your fingers.

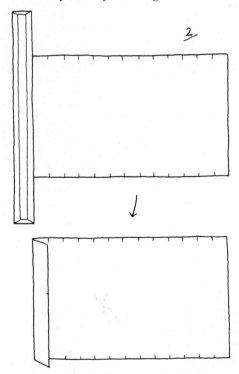

3. Turn the paper over and lay the rule to match the second set of marks. Press the rule down firmly then lift the paper to form a crease. Remove the rule and

press the crease as before. Continue to turn and crease until the full concertina has been formed.

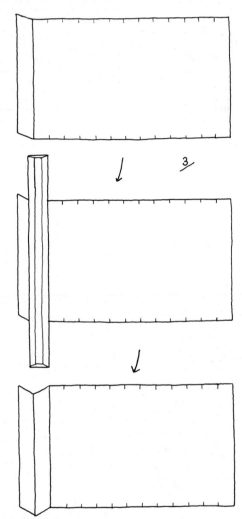

4. Stick a strip of DSST to each of the last two folds. Curl the concertina round and stick the two sides together.

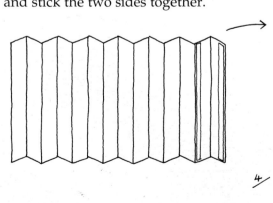
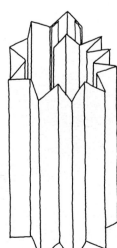

106

Creasing or perforating add a new dimension to the candle shades.

5. Other sequences of folding can be used. The more elaborate creasing methods will require a longer piece of paper – two pieces can be joined to make side seams.

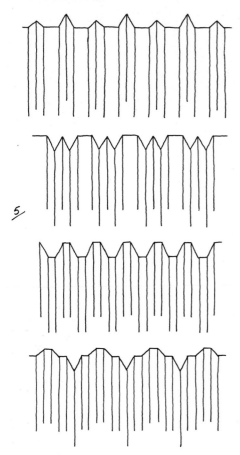

Perforated shade

Any shapes can be cut from the paper, so long as the structure of the shade is not weakened. I chose this one because the paper (rather thin, hence the strengthening circles at the top and bottom) has a fine diagonal indentation. The cut-out strips are at right angles to the indentations. You do not need to be a mathematical genius to work out the more geometric arrangements, but working out ideas on identically sized paper is important. Graph paper is very useful for this as it reduces the necessity for repeated measuring. Try to make sure that cut-outs are balanced at the top and bottom, i.e. avoid half- or quarter-cuts (see the drawing). Also,

make the bottom border slightly deeper than the top border because optically, if they are equal, the bottom border will appear to be narrower.

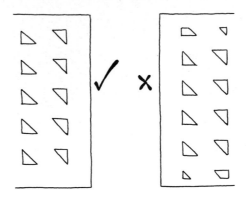

I generally prefer diffused light rather than a visible flame. This is achieved by covering the holes with drafting film, either small pieces, cut larger than the hole and neatly attached to the inside of the shade with DSST or, as in the case of the example shown, a full lining of the film. The lining film should be 3 to 4mm ($^1/_8$in) narrower than the width of the shade. Slip the lining inside the shade, matching the two seams. The lining should fit snugly against the shade; there is no need to stick them together.

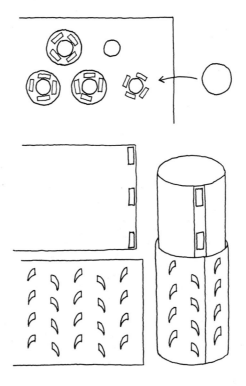

Chinese lanterns

The paper used for these is a rough, smooth laid. (The term 'laid' is used in the manufacture of commercial papers, in particular for types of writing papers. The horizontal marks on laid papers are produced by the close parallel wires on which the paper pulp is laid. The term 'smooth' refers to the actual surface finish of the paper). I have added the term 'rough' because the lines on this paper are not as regular or fine as those normally found on writing paper. As you can see, the glowing light gives a woody effect which, together with the slanting top, suggests a section of bamboo. Although the texture appears to be quite strong, the finish of the paper is in fact very smooth.

Each character denotes a charm (see caption). I intend to use these shades at my next Chinese dinner party and hope that my guests will be 'charmed' enough not to notice the foil take-away dishes in the waste bin!

To make the lanterns you will need: the list of materials given at the beginning of this chapter; paper (a laid writing paper would do – you will get one lantern from an A4 (8¼ x 12in) sheet, which is perfect for a normal candle jar but you will obviously need a larger sheet for a jam jar); a pair of compasses with an extension bar; a black felt-tipped marker with a brush tip (these are usually sold as a twin-ended pen – one end has a fine, firm tip and the other has a more flexible brush-like tip); tracing paper; 2H pencil; masking tape or some other low-tack adhesive tape.

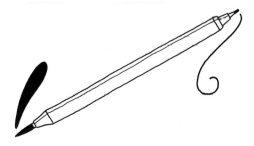

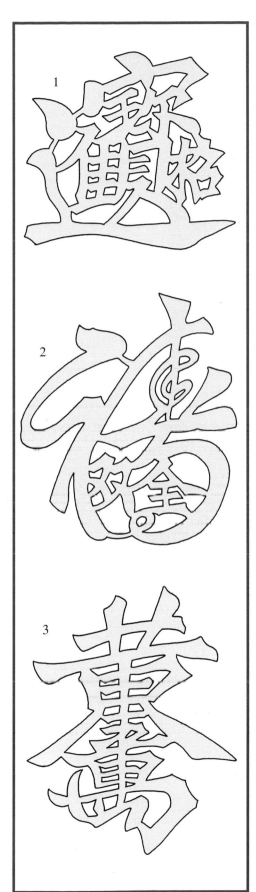

Chinese calligraphy is exquisite in its perfectly controlled but seemingly spontaneous brush strokes. Each of the three symbol shown right denotes a charm.

1. Chao Ts'ai Chin Pao is a charm to bring wealth.

2. Fu Shuang Ch'iian is a charm to ensure prosperity and long life.

3. Huang Chin Wan Liang will bring ten thousand ounces of gold.

109

1. Cut a rectangle exactly 180 x 270mm ($7^{1}/_{8}$ x $10^{5}/_{8}$in) and a strip 20mm ($^{3}/_{4}$in) wide and 273mm ($10^{3}/_{4}$in) long. Stick a piece of DSST along the strip.

2. Mark the centre of the rectangle and then make a pencil mark 15mm (just under $^{5}/_{8}$in) from the edge. Position the compass on that point and draw an arc which almost reaches the top of the rectangle. Carefully cut along this line using scissors or your craft knife – whichever you are more confident with. Rub out the pencil marks.

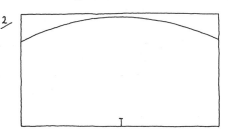

Candlelight illuminates the Chinese calligraphy hidden inside these candle shades. Each symbol represents a good-luck charm.

3. Lightly draw a vertical line 75mm (3in) from the side edge and another 60mm (2³/₈in) from the bottom edge.

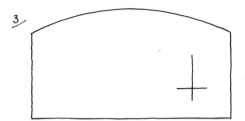

4. Carefully trace one of the charms using a very sharp HB pencil. Keep sharpening the point as it wears down. Turn the tracing paper over and position it in the centre of the vertical line and resting on the horizontal line. Use small pieces of low-tack tape to secure the tracing paper (or rub most of the tackiness from the masking tape to prevent damage to the paper).

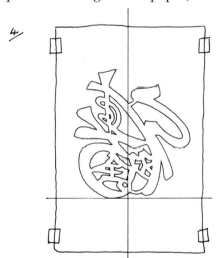

5. Using the 2H pencil, draw over the original lines of the symbol. Carefully remove the tracing, making sure that the tape does not tear the paper. Using the brush pen, fill in the lines.

6. Turn the paper over and stick a strip of DSST down the right side. Curl the paper round and stick the two sides together (see page 105).

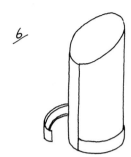

7. Matching the back seam, attach the strip of paper round the base of the shade. You may have to trim off a fraction at the end.

Bedroom shade

Paper doilies were cut up to provide the silhouette and decoration for this shade. I used gold doilies for the inside (these give a much stronger image) and the usual white doilies for the outside trimming at the top of the shade. The paper is slightly textured and fairly stiff. The shade can be made from a sheet sized to accommodate the doily design.

Three candle jars fit neatly inside, two in the curves of the heart and one at the front. Doilies vary so much in size and shape that it is impossible to be exact about the final design; so use your own skill and imagination to produce a pattern. (I find that doilies with circular sections are easier to manipulate.)

The only glue required for this shade (apart from DSST for the seam) is the dry adhesive sheets. Anything else would be impossibly messy. It is rather expensive but very economical: nothing is wasted, you simply lay your cut-out on the glued sheet, rub firmly then lift and position on your paper.

To make the shade you will need: the equipment listed at the beginning of this chapter; an A3 (12 x 16½in) sheet of paper; a packet each of gold and white doilies; a sheet of dry adhesive; a black felt-tipped pen.

1. Cut about 50mm (2in) from the top of your sheet, then score it in half using the blunt edge of your knife. Stick a strip of DSST down one side. Turn the paper over and lightly draw a line down each side, the same width as the DSST.

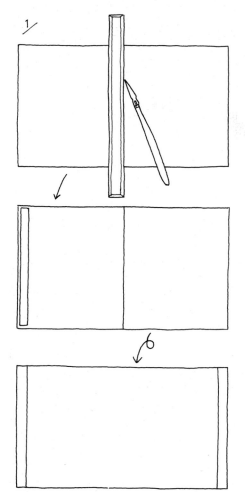

2. Having chosen your doilies, look to see which sections might produce an interesting design. Cut the gold pieces out and move them round until you get a good arrangement – avoid putting anything beyond the two pencil lines.

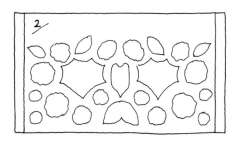

3. When the pieces are arranged to your liking, glue the white side to the paper. Using the black pen, join the sections together with small twig-like lines so that the design becomes one, rather than a collection of isolated pieces.

4. Turn the paper over. Arrange and stick white sections along the top edge. Carefully cut the edge, following the curved shapes formed by the sections.

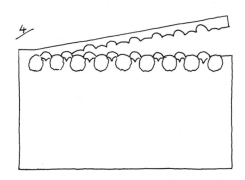

5. Carefully bend the paper round and stick the two sides together to form the shape of a heart.

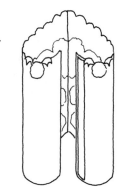

Mediaeval minstrel shade

These little minstrels were inspired by an illustration from the 1918 edition of the children's *Playbox Annual*, which has graced my bookshelf ever since I can remember. The artist was none other than the talented Heath Robinson.

The shade could be used at a children's party during the ceremony of blowing out the cake candles. It could also be used as a special bedtime treat when a fairy story is being read – needless to say, you should remove the candle when leaving the room.

Lack of space prevents a full-scale drawing of the castle. The original is twice the size of the plan given on page 114 so redraw it at a larger scale, or you could try enlarging it on a photocopier.

The paper I used is a pale brick colour, slightly grained and fairly stiff. Some art and craft shops may supply similar paper; if not, a tinted cartridge will do just as well. The steps are stuck on to the outside of the castle. Only these are seen until the candle is lit, then the playing minstrels become visible.

Paper doilies and mediaeval minstrels, hearts and castles, they are all good subjects for candle shades.

113

To make the shade you will need the materials listed at the beginning of this chapter, plus: a large sheet each of tracing paper and graph paper (if you are going to scale up the drawing; a dark-green felt-tipped pen (I used the twin-ended type described in Chinese lanterns. After tracing, the outline of the figures was drawn with the fine, firm tip, then filled in with the brush tip which gives a smoother, denser finish); 2H pencil; a sheet of dry adhesive (see also page 111.

1. Draw the castle on your graph paper; remember that everything needs to be twice the size.

2. Trace the castle on to your paper. The steps should be traced onto the castle, back and front (to use as a positioning guide). Cut out the castle, shape and the individual windows.

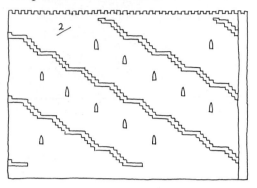

The diagram of the castle below is reproduced at half the original size. Enlarge by 200 per cent on a photocopier, or scale up on a larger sheet of graph paper.

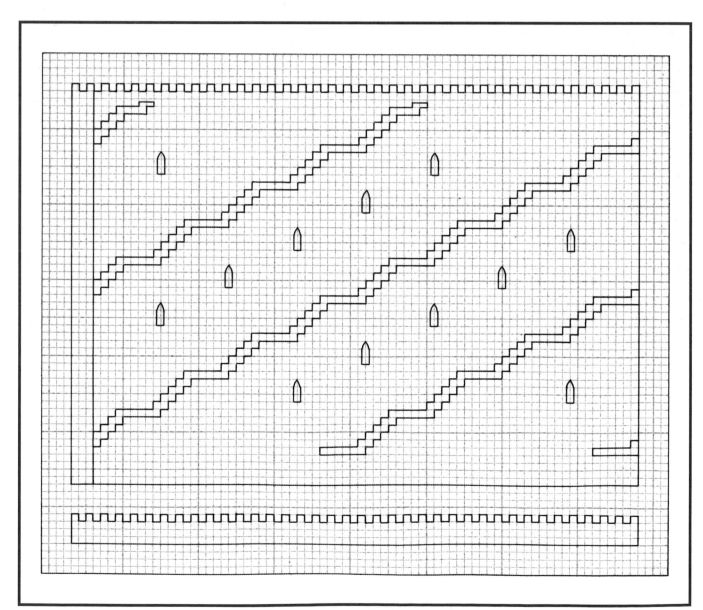

3. Cut out the strip for the bottom edge of the castle.

4. On a separate piece of paper trace all the step segments and cut them out.

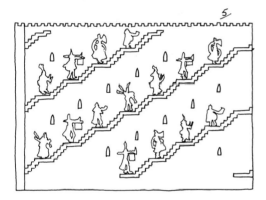

5. Using the full-size pattern opposite trace the little figures on to the reverse side of the paper.

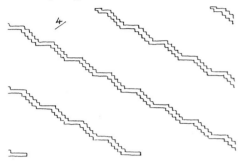

6. Fill in the outline of the figures using the green pen.

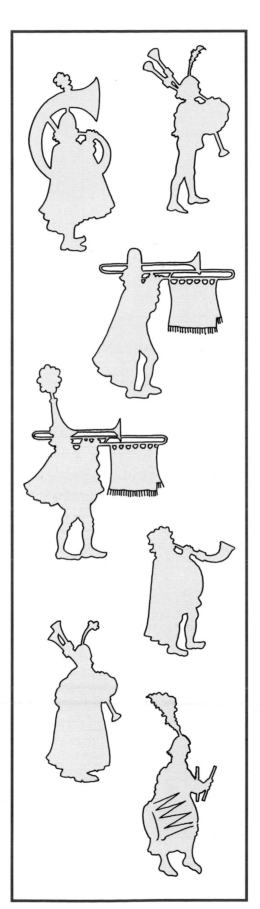

The patterns for the little figures are full size. I have drawn plumes on the minstrels' hats but I did not include them on the shade – the choice is yours.

7. Using the full-size diagram below trace the window covers on to tracing paper (twelve in all) and then cut them out.

8. Using small strips of DSST attach the window covers over the window cut-outs – on the reverse side of the paper.

9. Attach small pieces of DSST or dry adhesive to each of the step segments.

10. Following the drawn guide, attach the steps to the right side of the castle.

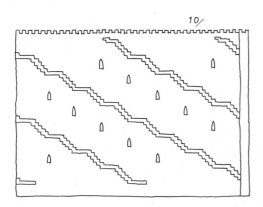

11. Stick a strip of DSST down one edge of the castle and carefully join the two sides together (see page 105).

12. Stick DSST to the bottom edge strip of the castle then, starting on the back seam, attach it all the way round. You may have to trim a little off at the end.

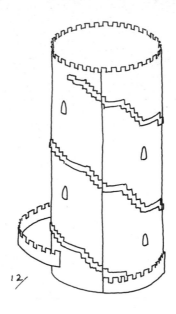

Spider's web

The rose outside my kitchen window was intended to ramble gently round the frame, giving a wistful, country-cottage feel to our suburban house. However, it had other ideas, one of which was to grow directly across the window, blocking out all light and encouraging strange insects. One morning I woke early and came down to find the most exquisite spider's web, hung with generous drops of dew... the inspiration for this candle shade.

To make the shade you will need the materials listed at the beginning of this chapter; an A3 (12 x 16½ in) sheet each of sturdy black paper, drafting film and clear acetate; an A4 (8¼ x 12in) sheet each of tracing paper and white paper; 2H pencil; white Conté crayon (like chalk but harder); glue stick; three different green tissue papers; silver poster paint; No. 2 paintbrush; felt-tipped marker; lighter fuel and cotton wool (commercial art clean is similar to lighter fuel but rather more expensive); sticky tape.

The finished spider's web candle shade complete with dew drops.

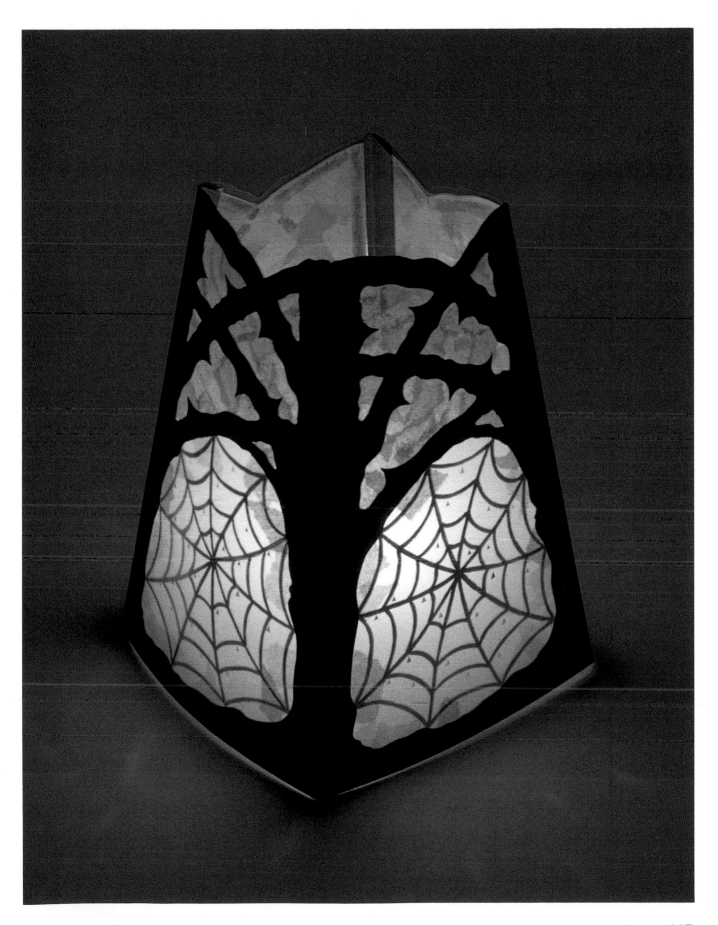

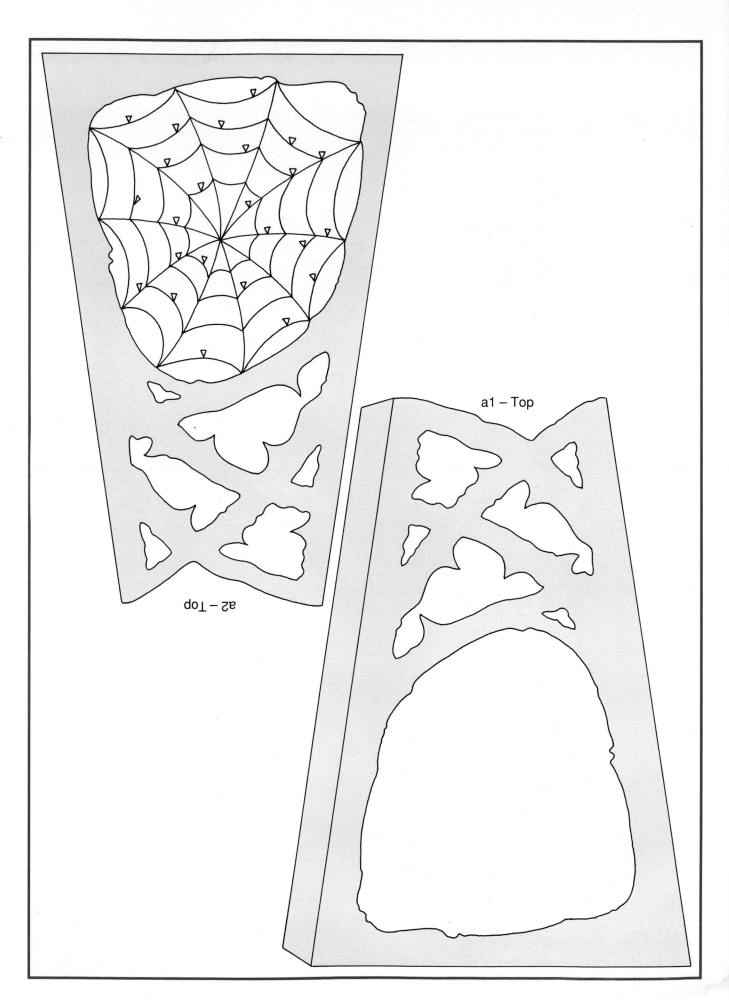

a1 – Top

a2 – Top

118

1. Cut the tracing paper in half. Using the full-size pattern opposite trace design (a1) on to one piece and design (a2) on to the other.

2. Turn tracing (a2) over, on to the white paper, and secure with pieces of sticky tape. Lay a piece of drafting film over the tracing and secure with sticky tape. Using your HB pencil, lightly draw the outer edge (as a guide for cutting) and the small triangles – the dew drops.

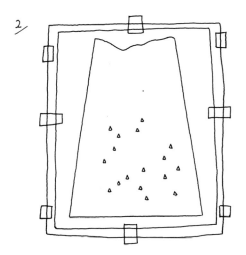

3. Start tearing small, irregular pieces of tissue paper and make a little pile of each colour. Using the glue stick, overlap the pieces on to the areas between the branches, then add a few round the edge of the web.

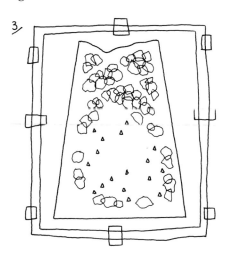

4. Remove the drafting film and, using your knife, cut out the little dew drops (erase any pencil marks.) Cut out the whole shape. With right side facing, stick strips of DSST round the edges.

5. Repeat the above steps 1 to 4 three more times then leave the four pieces on one side.

6. Turn the tracing (a1) over and rub the pencil lines with Conté crayon, blowing excess dust away. Lay the tracing on the black paper, secure with sticky tape and trace the design four times. Carefully cut out the inner sections, then the whole pieces. Lightly score the flaps with the blunt edge of your knife.

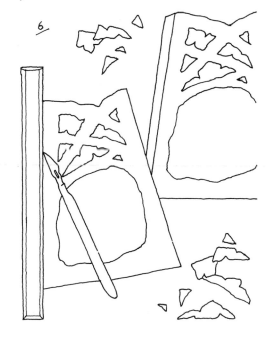

The pattern opposite, for the spider's web candle shade, is reproduced full size. Pattern a1 is for the main structure of the shade and includes a flap for joining the four pieces together. Pattern a2 is for the translucent image projected by the candle.

119

7. Turn each piece over and stick a few small strips of DSST along the branches. Carefully attach the drafting film, positioning it just in from the edge. (The side on which you stuck the tissue should be facing.) Repeat with the three remaining pieces.

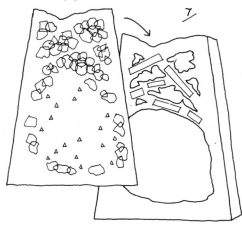

8. Stick strips of DSST round the edges of the drafting film and on the branches as before – hold the piece up the light to see where the branches are.

9. With tracing (b) still attached to the white paper, lay a piece of acetate over, securing with sticky tape. Wipe the acetate with lighter fuel and cotton wool. Draw round the outer edge of the design with the felt-tipped pen. Remove the acetate and cut out the shape. Carefully attach it to the drafting film.

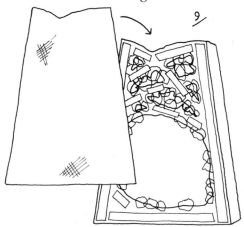

10. Lay the whole piece over the tracing. Secure with pieces of low-tack tape to prevent damage to the black paper.

11. Carefully paint the web with silver paint. In daylight the web will look white; the lighted candle turns the web into a silhouette and the flickering flame pierces the little triangles to give the effect of dew caught by the sun. Repeat with the three remaining pieces.

12. Stick strips of DSST down the flaps of each piece, right side facing, then join the four together.

Stained-glass shade

Coloured cellophane has been used to achieve the stained-glass effect in this three-sided shade. The process for making the shade is exacting – one needs to have dexterous hand-skills using the craft knife with very small pieces of cellophane and even smaller bits of DSST; patience is essential but this shade is well worth the effort.

I have included instructions for the design here, but you may want to start with something much simpler, which does not include quite so many small sections. Work your design out on graph paper. The width between the thick uprights can be based on the width of your DSST. The remaining design then falls between these thick strips and can be divided into various shapes and sizes.

To make the example shown you will need: the list of materials given at the beginning of this chapter; sheets or rolls of coloured cellophane; an A3 (12 x 16½in) sheet each of sturdy black paper; drafting film and clear acetate; stick of white Conté crayon; an A4 (8¼ x 12in) sheet of tracing paper; two similar-sized sheets of white paper; 2H pencil; low-tack sticky tape; pair of compasses; fine black felt-tipped pen.

Use this pattern full size for the stained-glass candle shade.

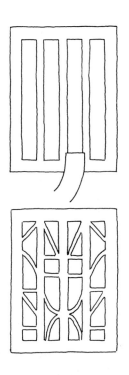

120

1. Trace the design on to the tracing paper, then turn it over and rub Conté crayon over the pencil lines. Blow off excess dust.

2. Attach the tracing, white side down, to the black paper, securing with low-tack tape. Trace the design.

3. Remove the tracing and carefully cut out the design. I find it easier to cut free-hand, without a steel-edged rule. Try this method on a spare piece of black paper, following straight and curved lines. (It is advisable to do the cutting over a long period to prevent acute soreness of the index finger!) Cut the whole shape out, scoring the flap with the blunt edge of your knife.

4. Carefully rub off any Conté crayon with your eraser. Turn the piece over on to a sheet of white paper and draw the design – this will be used as a cutting guide for the small pieces of cellophane.

5. Lay a piece of acetate over the original tracing, securing with sticky tape. Using the felt-tipped pen draw a line round the design, but 2mm (¹/₈in) larger. (If you use a compass to draw the arc, make a small wad with several pieces of sticky tape and place it over the centre

point. This prevents the compass needle from piercing the acetate).

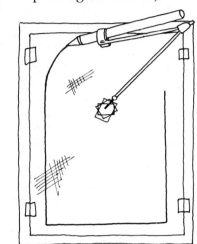

6. Remove the acetate and cut out the shape. With the reverse side of the black design facing, stick thin strips of DSST on the 'leading', then attach the acetate.

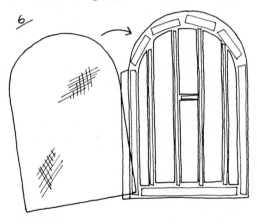

7. Stick the full width of DSST on to the acetate, cutting the top of each strip to follow the arc. Leave the backing on the DSST for the moment.

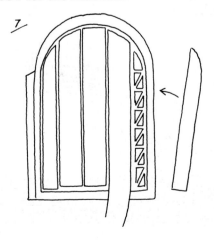

8. Using the white paper cutting guide, lay pieces of cellophane over each section of the left strip, hold firmly and cut to fit. When all the pieces have been cut remove the backing from the left strip of DSST and carefully stick on each piece, burnishing it with your knife handle to remove any little air pockets.

Coloured cellophane, drafting film and acetate help to create the stained-glass effect on this shade.

123

9. Continue in this manner until all the strips have been coloured. In order to achieve variation in density of colour, some sections will need another piece of the same colour. To apply these, cut thin strips of DSST and position round the section to be covered, then stick the cellophane on.

10. Now the whole area needs to be covered with drafting film (to diffuse the light). Use the original tracing as a template and repeat step 5, making the film slightly larger. Stick thin strips of DSST along the leading again, then attach the drafting film.

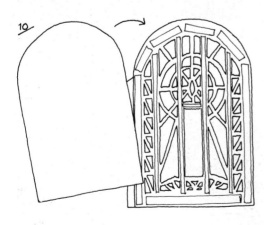

11. Repeat all the steps for the two remaining sides of the shade. Stick strips of DSST on to the flaps and join the three sides together.

124

Lemon-tree shade

Another way of achieving the appearance of stained glass is to use a transparent glass paint on acetate. The lemon tree was inspired by a Liberty block-printed cushion cover produced in 1904. The opaque background, which gives a nice contrast to the sharp, transparent colours of the tree, was made by mixing white with tiny amounts of blue, green and orange. The paint should be applied liberally, flooding it gently between the black outlines (black poster paint), rather than the usual method of painting with brush strokes. This is a four-sided shade and two of the sides are solid. I used this method of construction to give strength and to allow the candlelight to reflect the whiteness of the two sides.

To make the shade you will need the materials given at the beginning of this chapter; an A3 (12 x 16$^1/_2$in) sheet of mounting board (black one side, white the other); an A4 (8$^1/_4$x 12in) sheet each of acetate, tracing paper, plain white paper and thin white card; eight coloured transparent glass paints; glass-paint solvent; No. 2 paintbrush; black poster paint; small mixing palette; black felt-tipped pen; lighter fuel and cotton wool (see page 117.) The above items are all available from art and craft shops.

1. Cut the four pieces of the frame from the mounting board. The two solid sides measure 80 x 190mm (3$^1/_8$ x 7$^1/_2$in). The frames are 120 x 190mm (4$^3/_4$ x 7$^1/_2$in) with a 20mm ($^3/_4$in) border.

2. Using the black marker, blacken the side edges of each of the four pieces.

Lemon-tree candle shade.

3. Cut four 30 x 190mm (1³/₁₆ x 7¹/₂in) strips of thin white card. Draw a line exactly down the centre of each, then lightly score with the blunt edge of your knife. Using the black marker again, draw a line roughly 3mm (¹/₈in) wide to cover the scored line.

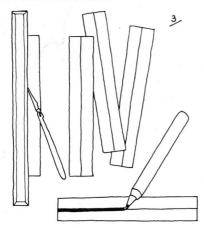

4. Cut four more pieces of the card, two at 19 x 76mm (³/₄ x 3in) and two at 19 x 119mm (³/₄ x 4¹¹/₁₆in). Stick a strip of DSST on the back of each.

5. Stick strips of 14mm (⁹/₁₆in) wide DSST down the sides of each piece (white side facing). Cut two pieces of acetate a little larger than the frames then clean both sides with lighter fuel and cotton wool. Carefully attach the acetate to the frames, turn them over and, using your knife, trim away the excess so that the acetate is flush with the frame. Stick strips of DSST, the same width as before, down each side of the frames. Do not remove the backing.

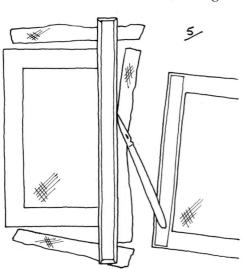

6. Trace the lemon tree design (page 127) on to tracing paper twice. Lay the tracing on to a piece of white paper and secure with tape. With the white side facing, secure each frame to the tracing.

7. Mix some black poster paint in your palette. The consistency should be wet, smooth and thick. Follow the outline of the designs. The first application will be streaky so repaint when the first coat is dry. (Practise on a spare piece of acetate first, until your line is steady and confident.)

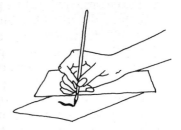

Always have a clean piece of paper to rest your hand on while working on the acetate – natural skin oils will prevent the paint from being properly applied.

8. Pour some white glass paint into the palette and add a little blue. Mix, then carefully flood the top area of both designs – take the paint up to the strips of DSST. Continue working your way down the fields, adding more white and specks of green, orange or blue to the original colour. Clean your brush with solvent then paint the leaves, carefully flooding both green and blue into each leaf shape. Repeat with brown for the trunk and yellow for the lemons, leaving a clear highlight at one side of each lemon. Leave the pieces to dry for two hours.

Full-size pattern for the lemon-tree shade.

9. Crease the four strips (corners) which have been scored. Remove all the DSST backing from the various pieces. Stick two corners to each frame, then the two longest of the four strips to the top of each frame.

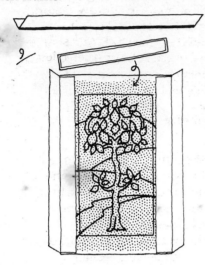

10. Stick the two solid pieces to the frames, then the two shorter strips to the top of each solid piece. The shade is now complete.